|汉英对照|

文明互鉴篇
CULTURAL EXCHANGES

中国
关

KEYWORDS
TO UNDERSTAND
CHINA

中国外文出版发行事业局(CICG)
当代中国与世界研究院(ACCWS)
中国翻译研究院(CATL)

朝華出版社
BLOSSOM PRESS

First Edition 2023

Compiled by
China International Communications Group
Academy of Contemporary China and World Studies
China Academy of Translation

Translated by
Du Nan, Song Hanyang and Wang Hairong
English text edited by
He Jun and Scott Huntsman (US)

Cover designed by
Du Shuai

ISBN 978-7-5054-5237-4

Published by
BLOSSOM PRESS
24 Baiwanzhuang Street, Beijing 100037, China

Distributed by
BLOSSOM PRESS
24 Baiwanzhuang Street, Beijing 100037, China
Tel: 86-10-68995532
Fax: 86-10-68995258
Website: www.zhcb.cipg.org.cn
E-mail: zhbq@cipg.org.com

Printed in the People's Republic of China

《中国关键词：文明互鉴篇》
图书编委会

Keywords to Understand China Cultural Exchanges Editorial Committee

前言

当今世界正经历百年未有之大变局，人类命运从未像现在这样休戚与共。不同文明包容共存、交流互鉴，在推动人类社会现代化进程、繁荣世界文明百花园中具有不可替代的作用。文明因多样而交流，因交流而互鉴，因互鉴而发展。在构建人类命运共同体的实践中，中国始终尊重世界文明多样性，秉持平等、互鉴、对话、包容的文明观，弘扬和平、发展、公平、正义、民主、自由的全人类共同价值，推动文明传承和创新，促进国际人文交流与合作，在“美人之美”的相互欣赏中走向“美美与共”的美好未来，为世界和平、稳定、繁荣注入文明力量、贡献中国智慧。

为讲好中华文明故事，介绍中国式现代化的文明根脉与精神力量，增进外国受众对人类文明新形态的了解，“中国关键词”多语对外传播平台组织策划了《中国关键词：文明互鉴篇》。本篇按照传统观念、历史活动、理念行动的编写逻辑，综合借鉴“中华思想文化术语传播工程”等有关成果，选取70多个关键词重点介绍和解读中华文明的精神价值观、源远流长的文明交流史、当代中国与世界文明互鉴，阐发中华文明讲仁爱、重民本、守诚信、崇正义、尚和合、求大同的精神特质和发展形态，展现当代中国的文明观。本书为中外对照版，由于能力及时间所限，在遴选编写中文词条时，难免挂一漏万。为使译文更符合目标语读者的阅读习惯，我们对翻译表达进行了创新探索，旨在提升读者的阅读体验。

“中国关键词”是中国外文出版发行事业局、当代中国与世界研究院、中国翻译研究院共同打造的国际传播品牌，主要围绕习近平新时代中国特色社会主义思想，进行中文词条专题编写、解读和多语种编译，通过平面、网络、移动端等多媒体、多渠道、多形态持续对外发布，旨在以外国受众易于阅读和理解的方式，阐释中国思想，解读中国理念，传递中国方案，分享中国智慧。

讲故事需要关键词，讲好中国故事需要中国关键词。让我们用“中国关键词”点击中国、沟通世界，促进中外文明交流互鉴。

Preface

The world is undergoing profound changes unseen in a century. More than ever before, we are living in an interconnected global village with a common stake. Inclusiveness, coexistence, exchange and mutual learning among different civilizations play an irreplaceable role in advancing humanity's modernization process and making the garden of world civilizations flourish. Diversity spurs interaction among civilizations, which in turn promotes mutual learning and their further development. In the process of building a global community of shared future, China has always respected the diversity of civilizations in the world by upholding equality, mutual learning, dialogues and inclusiveness between different civilizations and promoting the humanity's common values of peace, development, fairness, justice, democracy and freedom. In this way, we endeavor to push for inheritance and innovation of civilizations, facilitate international cultural exchanges and cooperation so that we cherish the beauty of each civilization and the diversity of civilizations in the world, with the ultimate goal of creating a better future for mankind by contributing China's strength and offering its vision to the peace, development and prosperity of the world.

Keywords to Understand China: Cultural Exchanges is launched by the China Keywords program, a multi-language platform for international communication, in a bid to tell the story of Chinese civilization, introduce the cultural roots and spiritual values of Chinese modernization, and enhance the understanding of China's new model for human advancement by the international audience. Drawing on the results of the Project on the Translation and Communication of the Key Concepts in Chinese Thought and Culture, it has selected more than 70 keywords to introduce and interpret Chinese cultural values, its long history of exchanges with other civilizations, and mutual learning between Chinese and other civilizations in the contemporary era, following the logic of presenting the traditional concepts first, reviewing the historical background and introducing the relevant ideas and action today. In this way, it tries to explicate the traits and development of the Chinese civilization and present Chinese cultural values, such as the notions of benevolence, humanism, integrity, justice, and coexistence in peace and universal harmony. The book is a bilingual version. Due to limited time and capacity, it is by no means an exhaustive list. We have done our best to make the translation of these keywords easy to understand and idiomatic for readers.

The China Keywords program is an international communication brand initiated by the China International Communications Group (CICG), the Academy of Contemporary China and World Studies (ACCWS) and the China Academy of Translation. Focusing on introducing Xi Jinping Thought on Socialism with Chinese Characteristics for a New Era, it edits and translates special Chinese concepts into different languages and releases them through multiple printed and online media platforms and channels, in a bid to explain and interpret Chinese thoughts and ideas, offer China's vision and share our wisdom.

To tell a story, we need keywords; to tell China's story well, we need keywords intrinsically associated with China. China Keywords are here to connect China with the rest of the world to promote mutual learning between Chinese and other civilizations.

目录
Contents

中华文明的精神价值观

The Values of Chinese Civilization

“向世界展现可信、可爱、可敬的中国形象”，有必要“讲清楚中国是什么样的文明和什么样的国家，讲清楚中国人的宇宙观、天下观、社会观、道德观”。为了促使世界读懂中国、读懂中国人民、读懂中华民族，向世界集中阐明中华文明的精神价值观，我们主要围绕“讲仁爱、重民本、守诚信、崇正义、尚和合、求大同”等中华文明的精神特质和发展形态，选择一些重要条目予以阐释。

"To present China as a country worthy of friendship, trust and respect," it is imperative to "explain what Chinese civilization is and what China is as a country, to shed light on Chinese views of the universe, of the world, of society, and of morality." To help people from other countries to have a better understanding of China, the Chinese nation and the Chinese people, we need to expound on the spiritual values that underpin Chinese civilization. This part will focus on "benevolence, humanism, integrity, justice, and coexistence in peace and universal harmony" to explain some of the most essential concepts that best represent Chinese civilization and its development.

孝老爱亲

孝老爱亲是中华民族的传统美德，意为孝敬老人、爱护亲人。“孝”字表达了中华儿女对父母孝养、孝敬的真挚感情，体现了全社会对老年群体的关爱和帮助。“爱”字道出了千万父母对儿女的真挚感情，也表达了千万儿女对父母养育之恩的真诚回报。“孝老”不仅包括物质上的供养，还包括精神上的慰藉。中国人非常重视亲人之间的情感，这种孝敬老人、爱护亲人的情感真挚纯粹、由心而发。

中华民族自古以来就重视家庭、重视亲情，倡导“老吾老以及人之老，幼吾幼以及人之幼”。家不仅是饮食起居的场所，还是亲情血缘的纽带，更是个体情感的归宿。孝老爱亲的道德观念生动表达了中国人深厚的家庭情结，反映了中国人浓厚的家文化传统。

Filial Piety for Parents and Affection for Kin

This concept captures the traditional Chinese virtue of respecting and caring for elders and loving one's family. Filial piety not only includes sincere affection and support for parents but also care for the elderly throughout all of society. Affection for one's kin is manifest in parents' selfless love of their children, and on the flipside, children's reciprocal gratitude to their parents and spontaneous actions to repay them. Filial piety requires both material and spiritual support. The notion reflects the importance Chinese people place on the emotional bonds between family members, especially genuine and spontaneous love among them.

An old saying goes, extend respect for seniors in one's family to those from other families and expand love for the young in one's family to other families. The Chinese nation fostered a tradition of valuing family and nurturing affection between family members. Family is not just a group of people living together; the concept features a strong emotional bond between members and a sense of belonging. This notion captures the Chinese people's deep attachment to family and reflects the importance of family as the basis of Chinese culture.

亲仁善邻

亲仁善邻出自《左传·隐公六年》，原文是“亲仁善邻，国之宝也”，意为亲近仁义之道，与邻国友好相处，这是国家的宝贵财富。中国古人认为，以仁爱、友善的态度对待他人的人，也能够受到对方同样的对待。中华民族历来爱好和平，主张以仁义之道对待其他国家的“王道”，反对以武力进行征伐的“霸道”。在这种理念之下，中国虽然在古代曾经长期领先于世界，却很少主动向周边国家实行征伐扩张，而是以安边为本、睦邻为贵。正因如此，古代中国以其高度发达的文明成就、仁爱友善的交往之道吸引了世界上很多国家和地区主动来华，开展长时段、大规模的政治、经济、文化交流活动，构成了人类文明交往史上的华丽篇章。

当代中国同样延续了这样的文明基因。与邻邦之间命运与共、守望相助，与不同文明之间交流交融、和平对话，是当代中国外交一贯的主张和做法，也是世界热爱和平的国家一致认同的理念。

Benevolence and Friendliness Towards Neighboring Countries

The original quote from *Zuo's Commentary on the Spring and Autumn Annals* (*Zuo Zhuan*) reads, "To be benevolent and friendly towards neighboring countries is a fundamental policy a country should pursue." Practicing benevolence and kindness towards neighboring countries is considered a state treasure. The ancient Chinese believed that treating others with kindness and friendliness would inspire reciprocal behavior. Chinese people have always cherished peace and advocated benevolence over hegemony or the use of force. For millennia, ancient China was more advanced than the rest of the world, yet it rarely embarked on expansionist expeditions against neighboring countries. Most of the time it maintained a policy of pacification and friendship with its neighbors. For this reason, the highly developed civilization of ancient China facilitated a wide range of long-lasting political, economic, and cultural exchange with many countries and regions that left a profound mark on human history and civilizational interaction.

The same civilizational trait was passed on to contemporary China. China's diplomacy has always aligned with that of every peace-loving country, recognizing a shared destiny and advocating helping neighbors in need and promoting civilizational intermingling through peaceful dialogue.

敬业乐群

敬业乐群出自《礼记·学记》，原意强调求学者要专心于学业、和同学相处融洽；后泛指一个人要认真干好自己的本职工作，同时与他人友好相处，努力融入群体之中。

中国人自古以来就注重职业道德，倡导“众志成城”“群策群力”，“敬业”“乐群”被视为职业道德的核心内容。“敬”是一种专心致志、心无旁骛的心理状态，以这种状态投入工作，才能不断提升职业技能，更好地实现自我价值。“乐群”意味着一个人应当积极融入集体生活，在与他人的相互协作中实现共同目标，而不是离群索居、自我封闭或单打独斗。在当代中国，“敬业”是社会主义核心价值观在个人层面的一个具体要求，“乐群”的精神有利于社会的团结与和谐。

Be Professionally Dedicated and Sociable

This notion first appeared in *The Book of Rites* (*Li Ji*). Originally, it stressed that students should immerse themselves in learning and develop fraternity with fellow students. Later, usage expanded to a more general sense to mean that a person should work diligently while developing friendly relations with others.

The Chinese have a long tradition of valuing professional ethics through emphasis on the strength of unity and stressing the importance of pooling the wisdom and efforts of everyone at work. Dedication to work and team spirit are considered the core of professional ethics. Only wholehearted devotion to work will empower a person to constantly improve their professional skills and better realize self-fulfillment. At the same time, being sociable at work requires a person to actively fit in the group and strive to achieve common goals in coordination with others rather than staying isolated or toiling alone. In contemporary China, being professionally dedicated reflects core socialist values while being sociable at work facilitates social unity and harmony.

博施众利

博施众利出自《论语·雍也》，意思是要广泛地帮助他人，给更多人带来好处。孔子（前551—前479）的弟子子贡问：“假若有这么一个人，广泛地给人民以好处，又能帮助大家生活得很好，怎么样？可以说是仁道了吗？”孔子回答：“哪里仅是仁道！那一定是圣德了！”可见孔子高度肯定利他行为。孔子主张“泛爱众”，即突破亲情血缘限制，去关爱更多的人。孟子（约前372—前289）主张“达则兼善天下”，同样表达了中华民族崇尚博施众利的品德和胸怀。

博施众利本质上是一种利他观念，其理念基础是自己与他人在根本意义上是一个整体，因此就不应过分强调二者的分别，而是要明白帮助他人也就是成就自己。中国坚定不移走和平发展道路，倡导互利共赢、合作发展，积极发挥负责任大国的作用，帮助第三世界国家的经济发展与社会进步，正是“博施众利”思想的体现。

Deliver Big Benefits for the People

As it appears in *The Analects of Confucius* (*Lun Yu*), this notion emphasizes the necessity of a ruler extensively helping his people and bringing them as many benefits as possible. One of Confucius' disciples Zigong asked: "If a ruler delivers extensive benefits to his people, how do you rate him? Do you consider him benevolent and virtuous?" Confucius (551-479 B.C.) said: "Not only is he benevolent and virtuous—I would call him a sage!" Confucius esteemed altruistic deeds. He urged people to love indiscriminatingly, regardless of kinship or blood, advocating "universal love." Mencius (c. 372-289 B.C.) exhorted successful individuals to dedicate themselves to the wellbeing of society—more highly influential Chinese philosophy on universal love that could benefit all humankind.

Essentially, *Deliver Big Benefits for the People* is an altruistic philosophy based on the idea that *me* and *others* are fundamentally a whole. Rather than divorcing the two, individuals should seek to help others succeed because it advances their own interests as well. China has steadfastly pursued peaceful development and maintained commitment to mutual benefits and development through cooperation. We earnestly fulfill our role as a responsible major country by supporting third-world countries in their socio-economic development, demonstrating this very concept in action.

民为邦本

民为邦本出自《尚书·五子之歌》，原文是“民惟邦本，本固邦宁”，集中体现了中华文明“重民本”的传统思想。“邦”意为国家，“本”原指草木的根部。枝叶的生长与繁盛，要靠根部吸收养分，因此根部是草木欣欣向荣的保障。与此类似，国家的维系和绵延要靠民众的支持和拥护，因此民众（而非神灵或君主）才是国家政治的根本。

孟子提出“民贵君轻”，认为民众在政治上比政府或君主更为重要。唐太宗（599—649）把君主比喻为船，把百姓比喻为水，借水既能让船得以航行，也能把船打翻的事实，形象地说明民众既可以支撑君权的运行，也能够让君权陷入覆灭的深渊。中国古代政治还强调“惠民利民，安民富民”，认为保障民众基本物质生活、增进民众福祉、维护社会稳定是执政者的重要责任。

基于民本传统，中国共产党把“人民至上”作为根本立场，坚持以人民为中心的发展思想，践行全心全意为人民服务的根本宗旨，这正是对中华民本传统的发扬。

People as the Foundation of the State

The original text of *Min Wei Bang Ben* first appeared in the *Book of History* (*Shang Shu*). "The people are the roots of the state," it reads. "Only if the roots hold firm can the state be stable." *Ben* refers to the roots of grass and trees. The growth and prosperity of the state are compared to branches and leaves which depend on nutrients absorbed through the roots. A sound root system guarantees a thriving plant. Similarly, the support of the people is essential for a state to stand firm and a regime to persist. It designated people, rather than gods or monarchs, as the foundation of a nation's politics.

Mencius declared that "people outweigh the monarch" while illustrating why people are more important politically than the government or monarch. Emperor Taizong of Tang (599-649) compared the monarch to a boat and the people to water. Water can float a boat, but it can also overturn and ruin it. Ancient Chinese politicians also stressed the need to "let people receive benefits, feel safe, and be better off." Protecting the people's livelihood and wellbeing and maintaining social stability were seen as the principal responsibility of rulers.

The Communist Party of China has staunchly embraced a fundamental position of "people first," anchored its development philosophy to the people, and delivered on its fundamental purpose of serving the people wholeheartedly in the spirit of the traditional notion of "putting people first."

为政以德

为政以德出自《论语 · 为政》，原文是“为政以德，譬如北辰，居其所而众星拱之”。孔子认为，如果从政者能够依据道德原则治理国家，那么他就会像北极星一样安居于中央，百姓则像其他星辰一样心悦诚服地环绕着他运行。这是孔子对于治国理政基本原则的具体论述。孔子强调，人心向背是国家治理的基础，而道德能够发挥持久的凝聚人心的作用。具体而言，“德治”思想包括两方面内容：在治理方式上，强调从政者应该顺应民意，施行仁政，维护人民利益，增进人民福祉；在个人修养上，强调从政者应该注重培养自身道德品质，以身作则，形成道德感召力，从而被人民所信服。此后，“德治”成为中国古代政治思想的主流，对中国政治和文化的发展产生了深远的影响。

当代中国治国理政的基本理念中，同样重视以德治国，强调依法治国和以德治国相结合，并且高度重视政府官员的道德操守，将“明大德、守公德、严私德、立政德”作为对政府官员的基本要求。

Governance Based on Virtue

Wei Zheng Yi De compared "governance based on virtue to the North Star holding its fixed position in the sky while all the other stars revolve around it (*The Analects of Confucius*)." According to Confucius, the people will orbit around the ruler like stars around the North Star if he governs based on virtue. This idea is the foundation of Confucius' views on governance. He emphasized that rallying support from the people is central to governing a country, and that virtue significantly helps bring people's aspirations together. "Virtue-based governance" can be broken down into governing style and personality traits. Good style involves heeding the public and responding to their concerns, exercising benevolence, protecting the people's interests, and promoting their wellbeing. Ideal personality traits include the ability to cultivate good moral qualities, set good examples, and gain trust from the subject people. "Governance based on virtue" became the mainstay of ancient Chinese political thought, and its influence remains profound and enduring.

Contemporary China also accentuates the importance of virtue in state governance, emphasizing the combination of law-based and virtue-based governance. Besides, government officials are required to have political integrity, observe the code of conduct in public office, apply high moral standards in their private lives, and maintain political commitment.

讲信修睦

讲信修睦出自《礼记 · 礼运》，意为讲究诚信，谋求和睦。这是中国古人所描述的“大同”理想社会的重要特征之一，即人与人之间、国与国之间彼此信任合作，和睦相处。此后，讲信修睦成为中国文化中处理人际关系和国际关系的一个重要准则。

“信”是中国传统的五种核心价值（仁、义、礼、智、信）之一，其基本含义是信用、信任、诚信。从普遍意义上来讲，诚信是任何社会存在的基础性原则，如果社会成员之间缺乏最基本的信任，那么这样的社会是无法长期稳定存在的，公共生活更加无从谈起。以诚信为基础，社会成员之间才可能建立和睦、友善的人际关系，开展良好的公共生活，形成社会共同体。

诚信是当代中国社会主义核心价值观的重要内容，也是开展国际交往的重要原则。中国坚持亲诚惠容理念，深化同周边国家互利关系；秉持真实亲诚理念，加强同发展中国家团结合作。国际社会也应坚持诚信的基本原则，以诚相待、和睦相处、互信互利、合作共赢。

Maintain Good Faith and Pursue Harmony

The term *Jiang Xin Xiu Mu* from *The Book of Rites* refers to practicing good faith and seeking harmonious relations, a vital feature of the "universal harmony" in society envisioned by the ancient Chinese. In an ideal society, people and states forge mutual trust, cooperation, and harmonious relations with one another. It later became an important Chinese cultural norm for governing people and state relationships.

Xin, or faith, is one of the five core values of the Chinese tradition (alongside benevolence, righteousness, propriety, and wisdom). It connotes trustworthiness, integrity, and honesty. More generally, honesty is a fundamental principle for any society. An absence of mutual trust and integrity among its members will eventually cause instability in society, making it impossible to carry out public life. Honesty and harmonious and friendly interpersonal relations are the key components of good public life and essential for construction of a social community that benefits all members.

Good faith is a crucial element of the core values of contemporary Chinese society and a major principle in international exchanges. China practices amity, sincerity, mutual benefit and inclusiveness to deepen its mutually beneficial relations with neighboring countries. We uphold sincerity and honesty and seek to strengthen solidarity and cooperation with developing countries. The international community should also champion good faith, treat others with sincerity, promote living in harmony, and seek to achieve win-win cooperation through mutual trust and mutual benefits.

知行合一

知行合一是明代思想家王阳明（1472—1529）提出的重要思想。中国古代哲学有大量关于知行关系的讨论，有知先行后、知易行难、知先行重、知行并进、知行合一等多种说法。王阳明从道德意识和道德行为的角度探讨知行合一，认为认知和实践是密不可分的，要达到知，就必须通过行；同时，知决定行，行要以知为指导。他主张道德意识和道德行为互为表里，内有良知则外有良行。他反对把知和行分开看待为由此及彼的关系，反对在道德方面的知行脱节、知而不行。

知行合一的哲学思想是对中国思想史上知行观的继承和发展，它赋予人以主体性的积极意义，为人们认知与实践提供了一套价值判断的标准，即知是基础、前提，行是重点、关键。今天，人们多用“知行合一”强调理论与实践的统一。

Unity of Knowledge and Action

This important notion was proposed by Wang Yangming (1472-1529), a Chinese philosopher of the Ming Dynasty. Many have discussed the relationship between knowledge and action in ancient Chinese philosophy. The relevant axioms are many, including "first knowledge, then action," "to know is easy, to act is hard," "knowledge comes first but action is more important," "knowledge and action develop together," and "unity of knowledge and action". From the perspective of moral consciousness and moral behavior, Wang Yangming argued that knowledge and action are inseparable and that action begets knowledge. At the same time, knowledge determines action, and action is guided by knowledge. According to Wang Yangming, moral consciousness is manifest in moral behavior because one's innate moral knowledge necessarily leads to good behavior. He argued against the separation of knowledge and action and criticized those who know but do not act.

This notion is an evolution of the concepts of knowledge and action in the history of Chinese philosophy. It stresses the subjectivity of human beings and offers criteria for judging knowledge and action: knowledge forms the foundation and prerequisite for action, while action is the key to knowledge. Nowadays, the notion is often used to emphasize unity of theory and practice.

扶危济困

扶危济困出自《水浒全传》，意为扶助面临危难的人，救济陷入困苦的人。扶危济困是中华民族的传统美德。先秦典籍《尚书》告诫执政者，不要虐待那些鳏寡孤独求告无门的人，不要抛弃困苦贫穷无所依靠的人。孔子提出，君子应当帮助有急需的人，而不是本来富有的人。墨子（约前468—前376之间）希望人们爱人如己（兼相爱），主张有力气的人尽力帮助他人，有钱财的人努力分给他人，有知识的人勉力教育他人，才能让饥饿的人得到食物，寒冷的人得到衣服，从而结束混乱，实现善治。中国民间谚语中还有"与其锦上添花，不如雪中送炭"的形象说法。扶危济困不仅是一种外在的义务或责任，更是对他人困难感同身受的同情心。扶危济困不仅能帮助他人渡过难关，还能给施助者带来内心愉悦。

基于扶危济困的传统美德，中国人培养形成面对困难时团结互助的精神。近年来，中国共产党和中国政府推动全社会践行社会主义核心价值观，传承中华民族守望相助、和衷共济、扶贫济困的传统美德，引导社会各界关爱贫困群众、关心减贫事业、投身脱贫行动。经过不懈努

Save Those in Danger and Help Those in Hardship

This concept originated in the *Outlaws of the Marsh* (*Shui Hu*). As a traditional virtue, the idea is reflected in many Chinese classics. For example, the *Book of History*, a pre-Qin classic, advised the ruler to avoid oppressing the helpless or neglecting the poor. In *The Analects of Confucius*, the sage declared that a gentleman helps the distressed instead of further enriching the rich. In his eponymous book, Mozi (c. 468 - 376 B.C.) advocated universal love. "Let him who has strength be alert to help others, let him who has wealth endeavor to share it with others, and let him who possesses the Dao (Way) teach others persuasively," he wrote. "In this way, the hungry will be fed, and the cold will be clothed.When tumult is brought to an end, sound governance will be secured." A more vivid expression of the idea is captured in the Chinese proverb, "Better send charcoal in snowy weather than add flowers to a brocade." The notion not only stresses a sense of responsibility but also expresses sympathy for those in distress. It gives the benefactor a sense of joy.

Influenced by this idea, the Chinese developed a spirit of unity and mutual assistance to navigate difficulties. In recent years, the Communist Party of China and the Chinese government have been promoting core socialist values in society to preserve and revive the traditional virtues of unity and mutual assistance as well as assistance to people in need, calling on people from all walks of life to get involved in the cause of poverty reduction and take concrete actions to help the im-

力，中国近1亿农村贫困人口全部脱贫，脱贫攻坚战取得了全面胜利，区域性整体贫困得到解决，完成了消除绝对贫困的艰巨任务，全面建成小康社会。这正是扶危济困精神在当代中国的生动实践。

poverished. Relentless efforts resulted in China securing a complete victory in the fight against poverty and welcoming a moderately prosperous society in all respects by lifting nearly 100 million rural population out of poverty, eliminating overall regional poverty, and eradicating extreme poverty, which now serves as a shining example of how the Chinese practice this traditional virtue.

见义勇为

见义勇为出自《论语 · 为政》，原文是“见义不为，无勇也”。孔子认为，见到正义的事情如果不去做，是没有勇敢之德的表现。由此演化出成语“见义勇为”，强调见到正义的事情就要勇敢地去做，这是中华民族的一项传统美德。

“义”是中国传统的五种核心价值（仁、义、礼、智、信）之一，其基本含义是合宜，引申为正义。“义”的标准是普遍公认的道德原则和社会规范，是对个人行为、思想的规范和引导。中国古代主流价值观有“义利之辨”，其实质就是对公益和私利的合理区分。任何一个社会都有超越于特殊个体利益之上的公共利益，这是维系社会共同体存在的基础，因此需要有相应的道德规范提倡、引导社会成员关心公益，甚至在某些情况下放弃个人私利。“勇”则是由“义”激发出的道德勇气。古往今来，中国无数仁人志士为了国家、社会和他人利益而勇敢地奉献出自己的一切甚至生命，维护了国家统一、社会稳定，推动了历史的发展。在当代中国，见义勇为是全社会大力提倡的主流价值观念和优秀品德。

Act Bravely for a Just Cause

This notion originated in *The Analects of Confucius*. "To see what is right and not to do it shows a lack of courage," goes the full quote. It stresses that a person should act courageously to do what is righteous. It is also considered a traditional Chinese virtue.

Yi (righteousness) is one of the five core values of traditional Chinese culture alongside benevolence, propriety, wisdom, and good faith. It essentially means "reasonable" and "proper," but was expanded to mean righteousness. The criteria for being righteous are generally accepted moral principles and social norms, which are used to regulate individual behaviors and serve as spiritual guidance. The mainstream values of ancient China demarcated a line between *Yi* (righteousness) and *Li* (gain). The essence is a reasonable distinction between the greater good and personal gain. In every society, some public interest must transcend special personal interests, which forms the foundation of the social community. Therefore, it becomes necessary to use moral codes to advocate for the public good among members of the society, sometimes at the expense of personal gain. Righteousness inspires bravery. Through the ages, countless Chinese people with lofty ideals sacrificed themselves for the greater good, whether it was to safeguard national unity or social stability, thus igniting historical progress. In contemporary China, the notion has become a mainstream value and consensus virtue in society.

和而不同

和而不同出自《论语·子路》，原文是"君子和而不同，小人同而不和"。孔子认为，君子能够与他人保持和谐友善的关系，但在具体问题的看法上则有自己的独立思考，不盲从附和；小人则相反。"和而不同"是孔子对人际交往基本原则的论述，也是中国古人对于世界多样性和统一性看法的精练概括。

"和"是多样性的调和与平衡，"同"则是把不同的事物转变成相同的。"和而不同"，就是尊重事物的差异性，并强调这些差异性恰好构成丰富多彩的整体世界。每一种事物存在于整体中，各自有其恰当的位置和价值，并与其他事物和谐共处，构成具有多样性的整体。"和而不同"理念体现了中国人的社会观，即以相互尊重的方式化解冲突，以求同存异的态度寻求共识，以彼此合作的精神和谐共存。

Harmony without Uniformity

This notion of harmony without uniformity originated in *The Analects of Confucius.* "The gentleman aims at harmony, and not at uniformity," reads the quote. "The mean man aims at uniformity, and not at harmony." A gentleman is affable with others, but he has his own views when it comes to a particular issue and will not follow others blindly. The opposite is true of the mean man. Harmony without uniformity is considered by Confucius to be a basic principle to guide interpersonal relations. It also epitomizes the ancient Chinese view on diversity and uniformity in the world.

Seeking harmony requires reconciling differences and striking a balance between them and promoting uniformity implies making everything identical. Harmony without uniformity connotes respect for differences and stresses that such differences make the world diverse. Everything has its place and value; things coexist harmoniously to make a diverse whole. This concept shines light on the social values of the Chinese people: They resolve differences based on mutual respect, seek common ground while acknowledging differences, and pursue harmonious coexistence through cooperation.

和实生物

和实生物出自《国语·郑语》，由西周末年太史伯阳父提出。在伯阳父看来，把不同的东西加以协调平衡叫作“和”。有差异的“和”才能生成万物，“和成”的物才能丰富发展，并令外物来归附聚集。如果仅仅把相同的东西予以叠加，是不能持续发展下去的。

“和实生物”意味着“生”是目的，“和”是实现“生”的方式，而差异性是“和”的前提。这一理念一方面尊重差异，另一方面又反对固化差异，从而充分看到具有差异性的各个要素相互作用、协调平衡，在时间延续中不断形成新的事物。基于这一理念，中国人乐于以正面的眼光看待发展变化，拥抱新生事物。中国主张以文明交流、互学互鉴，促进人类文明发展和社会进步，体现了和实生物的原则。

Harmony Begets New Things

This notion can be traced to *Discourses of the States* (*Guo Yu*). It was advanced by Court Historian Bo Yangfu during the late Western Zhou Dynasty (1046-771 B.C.). According to him, harmony means coordinating and balancing different things. Only by maintaining differences does harmony beget new things, which will then thrive by absorbing external elements. Progress cannot be sustained merely by combining things of the same type.

Therefore, harmony is even the strategy to accomplish the goal of begetting new things, with differences being a prerequisite. This idea promotes fostering respect for differences and opposes homogeneity. New things will emerge over time through various elements interacting, coordinating, and balancing each other. Influenced by this idea, the Chinese tend to look at changes in a positive way and embrace new things. This idea also underpins China's advocacy of cultural exchange and mutual learning to drive the progress of society and humanity.

协和万邦

协和万邦出自《尚书·尧典》对中国上古时期部落联盟首领尧（前30世纪—前21世纪之间）的一段描述，大意为尧能够弘扬品德，让氏族内部亲善和睦；继而处理各个氏族的事务，实现社会和睦；再协调各个邦国的关系，进而实现邦国之间和谐相处。

协和万邦是中国古代处理邦国之间关系的基本原则，也是中华文明一贯的处世之道。在当代社会，这一理念被运用于协调不同国家之间的关系，倡导世界各国相互尊重、和睦共处，实现共同发展。近年来，中国领导人多次提到协和万邦的国际观，倡导构建新型国际关系，体现了这一传统智慧的时代价值。

Harmony among All Nations

This notion is originally used to describe Yao, a legendary leader-chief of allied tribes referenced in ancient China in the *Book of History*. By promoting virtues and morality, Yao facilitated amicable relations within his tribe as well as between different tribes and achieved social harmony and coordinated relations between different states and thus harmonious coexistence.

Harmony among all nations is not only a basic goal guiding the diplomatic relations of ancient China, but a philosophy consistently promoted in the Chinese culture. In contemporary China, it is manifested in foreign policy of advocating mutual respect and harmonious coexistence among all nations for common development. In recent years, it has been cited several times by Chinese leaders as their position on international relations, demonstrating the contemporary relevance of this ancient wisdom, especially in terms of developing a new type of international relations.

天下为公

天下为公出自《礼记 · 礼运》，意为天下为天下人所共有。这是中国古人心目中“大同”理想社会的基本特征，与天下为一人或一家所有的私有制相对。“天下”是中国古代世界观的核心观念，其基本含义是“天”之“下”的所有土地和人民，即整个世界。

天下为公作为一种政治目标和社会理想，反映了人们对于社会公平、正义的要求，并且为人们提供了一种评价和改进现实世界的标准，突出反映并贯穿于近代以来中国革命和改革的历史进程中。这一理念启示我们，各国在谋求自身利益的同时，也应做到兼顾其他国家和整个世界的公共利益，以实现和谐共存、共同发展。

Everything under Heaven Belongs to the People

This notion originated in *The Book of Rites*. Contrasting the feudal idea that the state is property of the sovereign, it hypothesizes the ideal society of universal harmony envisioned by the ancient Chinese in which everything under heaven belongs to the people. "Tianxia," or "All-under-heaven," was a core concept of the traditional Chinese vision of the world order. It refers to all the land and people under heaven—literally the whole world.

As a political goal and social ideal, it not only serves the people's desire for social fairness and justice, but also as a gauge to evaluate and improve the real world. The ideal has featured prominently in numerous revolutions and reforms in modern China. It inspired the philosophy of a nation accommodating the interests of other nations and the world in the pursuit of its own to realize harmonious coexistence and common development.

天人合一

天人合一作为一个完整的词组最早出现在北宋张载（1020—1077）的《正蒙·诚明篇》中，但作为一种世界观和思维方式早已存在，其源头可以追溯到《周易》。天人合一是中华文明的宇宙观的重要内容，集中体现了对整个宇宙以及人与宇宙万物关系的根本看法。这一理念一方面强调整个世界的有机关联，认为人类与鸟兽、草木、山水都是宇宙的一部分，万物共生共存，共同构成宇宙这个最大的生命共同体；另一方面强调人在宇宙万物中具有特殊性，即人可以了解并利用宇宙规律，应该主动顺应和效法“天道”的生生不息，以仁爱之心对待天地万物，将天地万物视为同自己紧密相连的生命共同体，实现天、地、人的协调统一。

天人合一体现了中华民族的崇高追求和生态智慧。这一理念启示我们，应重新审视近代以来人类中心主义的自然观，改变对自然过度索取、破坏的发展模式，正确看待人与自然的关系，心存敬畏，取用有度，承担人类自身对自然万物的责任和义务，推动实现人与自然和谐共生、人类社会永续发展。

Harmony between Humanity and Nature

This notion of harmony between man and nature first appeared explicitly in *Rectifying the Ignorant, Truth and Enlightenment* (*Zheng Meng*) by Zhang Zai (1020-1077) of the Northern Song Dynasty (960-1127). However, the idea existed for a long time previously as a world outlook and a way of thinking and can be traced back to *The Book of Changes* (*Yi Jing*). An integral facet of the Chinese worldview, it shines light on people's basic understanding of the cosmos and their relationship with it. The idea stresses global unity, that human beings, alongside other living creatures, coexist with nature and constitute the cosmos, the biggest shared community of life. At the same time, it also recognizes the uniqueness of human beings for their ability to understand and exploit the laws of the universe. Thus, humans should follow the Way of Heaven, treat all in nature with benevolence, and recognize them as part of a shared community of life. This is the path to realization of harmonious unity of heaven, earth, and human beings.

This idea also reflects the lofty ideals and wisdom of the Chinese nation. It demands a review of anthropocentrism in modern time, changes to the development model that over-exploits and damages nature, and reverence for nature. It frames the human relationship with nature from a healthier perspective which promotes more efficient usage of natural resources. Humans must fulfil obligations to nature and actively seek harmonious coexistence with it according to the philosophy to achieve sustainable development in the human society.

道法自然

道法自然出自《道德经》。老子认为“道”不仅是天地万物的最初本源，而且是事物运动、变化的动力和规律，也是人生应当遵循的准则和规范。“道”高度尊重和包容它所创造的万物，并不干涉和控制万物，而是顺应万物的自然而然状态。

基于道法自然的理念，道家在政治领域主张执政者“无为”。“无为”并不是无所事事，而是要求执政者充分尊重民众的自主活动，不要以主观意志过多地控制或干扰民众。中国倡导创新、协调、绿色、开放、共享的新发展理念，强调尊重人民群众主体地位和首创精神，努力建设人与自然和谐共生的现代化，均体现了道法自然的传统智慧。

The Way Follows Nature

This concept was first outlined in *The Classic of the Way and Virtue* (*Dao De Jing*). According to Laozi, Dao (Way) is the original source of the ontological existence of all things and beings, the driving force and ruler of how things move and change, and the manager of rules and norms to be followed in life. The Way creates everything yet it does not intervene in or command anything. Rather, it shows great respect and tolerance for all things it has created and allows them to take their own natural course.

In the political sphere, the Daoists advocated non-action (Wuwei). Non-action does not mean doing nothing. Rather, it requires rulers to leverage the initiative of the people instead of imposing their will on them or interfering too much. Today, this Daoist wisdom is manifested in China's advocacy of a new concept of development featuring innovation, coordination, greenness, openness, and shared results, China's respect for the principal role and pioneering spirit of the people, and China's endeavors to build modernization characterized by harmonious coexistence between man and nature.

孝悌忠信

“孝、悌、忠、信、礼、义、廉、耻”合称“八德”，是中国传统文化重视的八种道德条目。由于汉字多四字连言的组合，所以又可以分为“孝悌忠信”和“礼义廉耻”两组道德观念。在“孝悌忠信”中，“孝”是指子女要尊重父母和长辈的意见，并履行赡养的义务；“悌”就是兄弟姐妹之间要相亲相爱，相互尊敬和谦让；“忠”在古代主要指臣子要尽心竭力地为君主服务，今天多指人民要真诚地热爱自己的祖国，也指一个人在工作中要做到认真负责，不能敷衍了事；“信”多用来表示做人要讲诚信，诚实地遵守与他人的约定或契约。在中国人看来，不忠不孝、言而无信是对一个人非常严厉的批评。

孝、悌是家庭伦理，忠、信属于政治和社会伦理，孝、悌是忠、信的基础。这些道德观念描述了人与人之间的良性关系，至今仍然深深影响着中国人的生活。

Filial Piety, Fraternal Duty, Loyalty, and Good Faith

The Eight Virtues of traditional Chinese culture are filial piety, fraternal duty, loyalty, good faith, propriety, righteousness, integrity, and shame. They are usually split into two sets of moral values because the Chinese prefer four-character expressions. In the first set (filial piety, fraternal duty, loyalty, and good faith), filial piety requires children to respect the opinions of their parents and elders and take care of them when they are old. Fraternal duty refers to love, mutual respect, and courtesy demonstrated among brothers and sisters. Loyalty mainly refers to the deep allegiance pledged by subjects to the monarch in ancient times. Today, it could be used to describe patriotism or a responsible employee. Good faith requires people to act credibly and honestly abide by an agreement or contract with others. In China, accusing someone of being unfilial or disloyal is considered particularly sharp criticism.

Filial piety and fraternal duty are generally family ethics while loyalty and good faith are political and social ethics, with the former serving as the foundation of the latter. These moral values, which aim to foster sound interpersonal relationships, are still deeply rooted in the life of Chinese people today.

礼义廉耻

“礼义廉耻”是中国传统“八德”的重要内容，属于政治和社会伦理范畴。出自《管子 · 牧民》的“礼义廉耻，国之四维”，指“礼”“义”“廉”“耻”是维系一个国家的四项重要道德原则，就像四根精神支柱。其中，“礼”是调节人际关系、维护社会秩序的行为准则和道德规范，不仅包括大量具体的礼制，更强调培养人们遵循礼的内在恭敬之心；“义”指面对是非善恶要坚持正确的判断，作出合理的选择，特别是要超越个人的一己私利，多承担集体或公共的责任；“廉”指克制自己的私欲和贪念，不占有或收取不属于自己的财物，避免贪污腐败，这通常被认为是对官员政德的基本要求；“耻”就是保持羞恶之心，如果做了违背道德原则的事，就会感到羞愧，要反躬自省、改过迁善，实现自我道德约束。说一个人轻薄无礼、无情无义、寡廉鲜耻，对他是一种很严厉的批评。

孝悌忠信、礼义廉耻探讨了人与人、人与社会的关系。这些道德观念代代相传，成为中国人价值体系的重要组成部分，潜移默化地影响和塑造着中华民族的精神气质。

Propriety, Righteousness, Integrity, and Shame

Propriety, righteousness, integrity, and shame, of the Eight Virtues of traditional Chinese culture, are categorized as political and social ethics. They were first introduced in the book *Guan Zi* as four moral bonds to sustain a nation, like four cultural pillars. Among them, propriety refers to a set of social norms and moral rules used to adjust interpersonal relations and maintain social order. It not only stresses many specific rites and rituals, but also cultivates reverence for them. Righteousness means acting upright when making decisions and choices, refraining from seeking self-interests, and taking on collective and public responsibilities. Integrity means restraining selfish desires and covetous thoughts, refusing to take property that does not belong to oneself, and avoiding bribery and corruption. It is usually considered a basic political virtue. Shame refers to a sense of guilt when one realizes that one's actions have violated commonly accepted morals and involves conscious self-examination and correction of one's mistakes in an attempt to seek moral enlightenment. Accusing someone of being shameless is considered sharp criticism.

The Eight Virtues address interpersonal relationship as well as the relationship between people and society. An integral facet of the Chinese cultural values, they are handed down from generation to generation, unconsciously shaping Chinese outlooks on life.

自强不息

自强不息出自《周易 · 乾卦 · 象传》，原文是“天行健，君子以自强不息”。中国古人认为，天体的运行刚健有力、生生不息，君子为人处世也应效法天体，力求进步，勤勉不懈，奋斗不止。这一理念反映了中国人积极向上、奋发有为的人生态度，展现了中华民族不畏艰险、乐观奋进的处世精神。

与世界上各大文明系统相比，中华文明的一个显著特点就是长久地保持乐观、奋进的处世精神，主张在当下和现实世界之中寻找并实现生命的意义。因此，在面对艰难困苦时，个人应充分发挥自身的主体性、能动性，通过自身的不懈奋斗摆脱困境，从而实现自我价值。在当代中国，自强不息的优良传统正是激励着中国人民自力更生、团结奋斗的精神力量。

Continuous Self-Improvement

This notion first appeared in *The Book of Changes* which stated, "Just as heaven keeps moving forward vigorously, a man of virtue should strive continuously to strengthen himself." The ancient Chinese believed that heavenly bodies moved in a vigorous and perpetually forward moving cycle. A man of virtue who follows the Law of Heaven should be fully motivated and work diligently to strengthen himself. This idea reflects the Chinese life philosophy advocating optimism, courage, and self-motivation.

The central traits of Chinese culture are a positive outlook on life and pursuit of self-fulfillment at present and in the real world. Individuals are encouraged to act on their own initiative and work diligently to overcome difficulties and achieve self-fulfillment. In contemporary China, the tradition of constantly seeking self-improvement still inspires and unites the Chinese people.

厚德载物

厚德载物出自《周易 · 坤卦 · 象传》，原文是“地势坤，君子以厚德载物”。意为大地宽广和顺、涵养万物，君子为人处世应像大地一样，以博大宽厚的德行包容万物。厚德载物体现了中国人自身修养与社会交往的信念追求。在中国人看来，一个人应修养自身德行，培养宽厚、包容、柔和的道德品格，尊重不同、维持多元，与他人和社会和谐相处。

自强不息、厚德载物构成了中华民族精神的基本品格。当代中国改革开放的进程，集中体现了这样的变革和开放精神。

Great Virtue Accommodates All Things

The idea of virtue accommodating all things originated in *The Book of Changes*. "The earth is generous and peaceful, and similarly, a man of virtue should have ample virtue and accommodate all things," it reads. This means that the earth, being generous and peaceful, sustains all things. Men of virtue should model themselves after the earth by caring for all things and fellow human beings with an open heart and virtues. The idea demonstrates the Chinese outlook on self-cultivation and social interaction. It instructs people to cultivate virtues of generosity, broad-mindedness, and mildness, respect differences and diversity, and seek harmony in relationships with others and society.

Alongside the notion of continuous efforts to strengthen oneself, it constitutes a fundamental trait of the Chinese nation which was fully embodied in pursuits of change and openness during the reform and opening up in contemporary China.

革故鼎新

革故鼎新出自《周易·杂卦》，原文是“革，去故也；鼎，取新也”。“革”是除去旧事物，“鼎”是建立新事物。“革故鼎新”意指破旧立新，推动事物发展和社会进步，其核心是适时变革、去旧更新。中国古人认为，永恒变化是宇宙万物存在的基本状态，因此应把握规律，适应变化，推动创新。这正是中华文明保持强大韧性和生命力的一个重要原因。

从古至今，中华文明之所以历久弥新、生生不息，就是因为它在坚持传统的同时，保持锐意进取的态度，与时俱进、开拓创新。中国历史上的商鞅变法、辛亥革命等，都是以破旧立新的改革精神探寻国家变革与社会进步之路，推动了历史的发展。当代中国秉承革故鼎新的精神，深化改革、扩大开放，创造了发展奇迹。革故鼎新已经成为中华文明永恒的精神气质。

Out with the Old and in with the New

The idea originated in *The Book of Changes*. "*Ge* signifies doing away with the old; *ding* symbolizes setting up the new," reads the full quote. It stresses the importance of timely changes to foster progress and social advancement. The ancient Chinese believed that the only constant in the universe was change. Thus, men should understand the law of the universe and adapt to changes to strive for innovation. This explains to a certain extent how the Chinese civilization has maintained strong resilience and vitality for so long.

A pioneering and enterprising spirit, which is deeply rooted in traditional Chinese culture, has provided an inexhaustible source of strength and vitality for Chinese civilization. Such a spirit is reflected in many historic changes through national reforms and social progress. Prime examples include the reforms of Shangyang (390-338 B.C.) and the Revolution of 1911. In contemporary China, the nation maintains the tradition by deepening reform and opening up, which has created many miracles of development. The idea of "out with the old, in with the new" has become a quintessential cultural trait of Chinese civilization.

居安思危

居安思危出自《左传·襄公十一年》，原文是“居安思危，思则有备，有备无患”。中国古人认为，即使处在安定的环境中，也要考虑到可能产生的危险，考虑到了就会提前做好防备，有防备就能避免祸患。正如《孟子》提出的“生于忧患，死于安乐”，人类历史上的无数事例已经反复证明了这一点。安定的环境最容易使人放松警惕而心生懈怠。然而，事物时刻处在发展变化之中，安定中也可能潜藏着危险的因素，如果不加以防范就会发展为巨大的祸患。因此需要时刻保持警惕，检视可能存在的危险，做好应对准备。

居安思危体现了中国人强烈的忧患意识。“思危”的目的在于能够长久地“居安”。无论对于个人、团体还是国家，只有时刻谨记居安思危，保持忧患意识，才能维持稳定的环境，获得长久的发展。

Be Prepared for Adversity and Danger in Times of Peace

This piece of advice originated in *Zuo's Commentary on the Spring and Autumn Annals*. "In times of peace, think of danger." it advises. "In your thoughts, you will be prepared, and once prepared, you can avoid calamity." The ancient Chinese believed that one should always be on alert for potential danger even in times of peace. Doing so ensures they will take precautions to avert danger. "Life springs from worries and hardship, and death from ease and pleasure," goes a line in *Mencius*. History has repeatedly shown that people can become complacent and let down their guard in times of peace and prosperity. However, things are in constant change, and latent danger is often hidden beneath peace and stability. If such danger is not recognized, it might grow into a calamity. Therefore, we should always stay alert and prepared for potential risks.

The concept reflects the strong Chinese awareness of potential risks. Only persistent vigilance can foster long-term stability and development. This is true with any individual, community, or nation.

俭约自守

俭约自守出自《素书》，原文是“恭俭谦约，所以自守”。意为做人要以勤俭节约来要求自己，这是中华民族的一项传统美德。基于天人合一的理念，中国人认为人类对自然的利用应该有所节制，不能滥用和浪费自然资源，否则会受到自然界的惩罚。俭约自守还关系到国家兴衰和家庭聚散。正如唐代著名诗人李商隐所说：“历览前贤国与家，成由勤俭败由奢。”在个人良好品德的养成方面，《左传》指出，节俭是有德之人共同的品质，而奢侈是恶行中的大恶。《周易》认为，君子能够通过节俭的美德避免灾难。

当今时代，科技的发展使得物质产品极度丰富，但人类不得不面临资源枯竭和环境恶化等问题；消费中心主义使人们追逐物欲的满足，但忽略了自身精神生命的成长和丰富。俭约自守体现了中国人认识和处理勤俭与奢华、集约与浪费之间关系的思想智慧。中国倡导“光盘行动”、全面加强资源节约工作、持之以恒正风肃纪反腐等，就是遵循俭约自守理念的具体实践。

Be Thrifty and Exercise Self-Restraint

This idea originated in *Su Shu*: "Be courteous and thrifty and exercise self-restraint." Thrift is a traditional virtue of the Chinese nation. Guided by the philosophy of harmony between humanity and nature, the Chinese believe that humans should refrain from excessive exploitation of natural resources, or nature will retaliate. Thriftiness and self-restraint can also directly influence the rise or fall of a family and even a nation. As Li Shangyin, a renowned poet from the Tang Dynasty (618-907), once wrote, "History tells us that diligence and thrift lead to success, while luxury and extravagance lead to failure." In terms of the cultivation of moral integrity, *Zuo's Commentary on the Spring and Autumn Annals* considers thrift a common trait shared by men of virtue and extravagance the biggest evil of all. According to *The Book of Changes*, "A gentleman avoids calamities by virtue of thrift."

In recent decades, advancement of technology has led to great material abundance. But humans now face resource depletion and environmental degradation. Driven by consumerism, people seek to satisfy their material desires, while neglecting growth and enrichment of the inner world. The idea of being thrifty and exercising self-restraint reflects the wisdom of the Chinese in understanding and handling the relationship between thriftiness and extravagance. Now, this idea is embodied in many Chinese policies such as the Empty Plate Campaign and the government's continuous efforts to conserve resources and fight corruption.

格物究理

格物究理由北宋哲学家程颐（1033—1107）提出，南宋哲学家朱熹（1130—1200）继承发展，意为考察事物，探究事物的道理，后用来表示考察研究事物的规律。

格物究理作为一种思想方法，探讨了认识与实践的关系问题。任何事物都有其固有性质和发展规律，要对相关事物进行详细的调查研究，真正了解其性质和规律，才能加以合理利用从而达到目的。格物究理讲求实事求是，与现代自然科学的精神具有相通之处，它的继承和发展有力促进了科学技术的发展，成为人们生产生活实践中都应遵循的基本方法。

Study in Quest of Principles

This concept, first proposed by the ancient philosopher Cheng Yi (1033-1107) and developed by Zhu Xi (1130-1200), originally exhorted people to study things to acquire principles. Later, it was used to describe inquiry of the principles of things.

As a way of thinking, it discusses the relationship between knowledge and application. All things have their own nature and law of development. Only through thorough inquiry of their nature and law can one make good use of them to achieve specific goals. Just like the natural sciences of the modern times, it stresses the importance of seeking truth from facts. The idea offers a basic approach to work and life, and its inheritance and development have effectively promoted progress in science and technology.

修身处世

修身处世，即修养好自身的德行，处理好与他者的关系，这一理念集中体现在儒家经典《大学》中。关于“修身”，《大学》强调，上自国家元首，下至平民百姓，人人都要以修养品性为根本。要做到修身，需要首先做好格物、致知、诚意、正心，就是要尽可能地研究清楚万事万物的道理，拓展自身的认知，进而让自己的意念真诚笃实、心思端正无邪。关于“处世”，《大学》提出了齐家、治国、平天下的次第，就是要为管理好家族、治理好国家、把和平与秩序带给天下作出应有的贡献。总体而言，修身是处世的根本和基础，一个人如果德行不好，很难处理好与他者的关系；处世也是修身的重要方法，一个人如果离群索居、远离他者，很难谈得上有意义的修身。

修身处世是中国人如何要求自己、对待他人的基本态度。在历史上，中国人积累了大量修身处世的智慧，赋予中华文明独特的自信、耐力与定力。

Cultural Moral Integrity and Good Conduct

This means that one should cultivate him/herself and manage interpersonal relations well. The idea is fully expressed in *The Great Learning* (*Da Xue*), a Confucian classic. According to the book, everyone from the ruler of a state to ordinary people should cultivate morality first by studying things, then acquiring knowledge, being sincere in thought, and rectifying one's heart. This empowers people to identify the principles of all things, expand knowledge, and then cultivate virtues such as uprightness and good faith. Then, the book offers the three steps to conduct oneself in society after achieving self-cultivation: manage one's family well, govern the state properly, and bring peace to all under heaven. In short, self-cultivation is the prerequisite and foundation for participation in society, and an important way to realize self-cultivation is by participating in society. A person lacking moral integrity cannot easily manage relations with others, and a person living in isolation can hardly achieve meaningful self-cultivation.

The concept reflects the general attitude of the Chinese towards self-cultivation and interpersonal relations. In history, the Chinese have accumulated considerable wisdom on how to cultivate moral integrity and conduct oneself in society, which injects confidence, endurance, and strength into Chinese culture.

源远流长的文明交流史

A Long History of Cultural Exchange

文明交流互鉴，是推动人类文明进步和世界和平发展的重要动力。源远流长的文明交流史告诉我们，只有交流互鉴，一种文明才能充满生命力。中华文明是在同其他文明不断交流互鉴中形成的开放体系。从历史上的佛教东传、“伊儒会通”，到近代以来的“西学东渐”、新文化运动、马克思主义和社会主义思想传入中国，再到改革开放以来全方位对外开放，中华文明始终在兼收并蓄中历久弥新。同样，世界其他文明也因交流而多彩，因互鉴而丰富。

Cultural exchange and mutual learning are important driving forces promoting human progress and global peace and development. The long history of cultural exchange shows that only exchange and mutual learning produce a civilization of vigor and vitality. Chinese civilization is an open system shaped through continuous exchange and mutual learning with other civilizations. From the introduction of Buddhism to China and mingling between Islam and Confucianism in history to Western concepts spreading East, the New Culture Movement, the introduction of Marxism and socialist thought to China in the modern times, and comprehensive opening up since 1978, Chinese civilization has always radiated dynamism by virtue of its inclusiveness. But it is true for all civilizations that culture becomes diverse through exchange and rich through mutual learning.

丝绸之路

丝绸之路，一般指陆上丝绸之路，是古代连接中西方的重要商道。在公元前138年的中国汉代，张骞出使西域，开始打通东方通往西方的道路。通过丝绸之路，商人们将中国生产的丝绸等运往中亚、西亚、欧洲和北非，再把欧洲和中亚等地的奇珍异宝输往中国。历史上的丝绸之路曾以长安（今陕西省西安市）、洛阳（今河南省洛阳市）为起点，经甘肃、新疆通往中亚、西亚，到达欧洲、北非，成为古代连接亚欧大陆的东西方文明交汇之路。

丝绸之路是古代多民族、多种族、多宗教、多文化的重要交往平台，促进了亚欧大陆各国互联互通，推动了东西方文明交流互鉴，为人类文明发展进步作出了重大贡献。1877年，德国地质地理学家李希霍芬在《中国》一书中第一次将这条西域交通道路命名为“丝绸之路”，这一概念由此广泛传播。随着时代发展，丝绸之路成为古代中国与西方各领域往来通道的统称。2013年，中国提出共建“丝绸之路经济带”重大倡议，得到国际社会高度关注和积极响应。2014年，中国、哈萨克斯坦、吉尔吉斯斯坦联合申报的陆

Silk Road

The Silk Road generally refers to the important overland trade routes linking China to the West in ancient times. During the Han Dynasty in 138 B.C., Zhang Qian embarked on a diplomatic mission to the Western Regions, opening a gate to the West. Along the routes, merchants carried Chinese silk westward to Central Asia, West Asia, Europe, and North Africa and brought back other high value goods. Historically originating in Chang'an (today's Xi'an of Shaanxi Province) and Luoyang (today's Luoyang of Henan Province), the Silk Road crossed Gansu and Xinjiang, traversed to Central Asia and West Asia, and reached Europe and North Africa, serving as a bridge for exchange between Eastern and Western civilizations.

By serving as an important platform for exchange between multiple nationalities, ethnic groups, religions, and cultures, the Silk Road has facilitated connectivity of countries in Eurasia and cultural exchange and mutual learning between the East and West, making major contributions to human advancement. The term "Silk Road" was coined by German geologist and geographer Ferdinand von Richthofen as recently as 1877 in his book *China*, and it was widely disseminated since. As time went on, the Silk Road was expanded to refer to all channels for exchange between China and the West in ancient times. In 2013, China proposed an important initiative of jointly building the Silk Road Economic Belt, which drew extensive attention and received strong endorsements from the international community. In 2014, Silk Roads: the Routes Network

上丝绸之路东段“丝绸之路：长安-天山廊道的路网”入选世界文化遗产。从开辟古代丝绸之路到今天共建“一带一路”，中国与丝路沿途各国友谊源远流长，历久弥坚，人文交流、经贸合作硕果累累。

of Chang'an-Tianshan Corridor, a joint application by China, Kazakhstan, and Kyrgyzstan, was listed as a World Heritage. From the ancient Silk Road to the Belt and Road Initiative today, China has built on traditional friendship with countries along the routes and achieved fruitful results in people-to-people exchange and business cooperation.

海上丝绸之路

海上丝绸之路是古代连接中国与世界其他地区的海上通道，它由“东海航线”和“南海航线”两大干线组成，形成于秦汉时期，兴盛于唐宋时期。海上丝绸之路东海航线从中国辽东半岛、胶东半岛通向朝鲜半岛、日本列岛直至东南亚，中国的商品被源源不断地输往这些地区，中国文化包括儒家思想、律令制度、汉字、服饰、建筑、武术、饮茶习俗等也得到大规模的海外传播。海上丝绸之路南海航线从中国广州、泉州通向东南亚、印度洋地区。从汉代开始，中国从东向西拓展海上丝绸之路，罗马帝国则自西而东航行，最后在印度半岛对接，从而使海上丝绸之路延伸到波斯湾、红海。这是世界历史上第一条跨越印度洋的海上航线，也是当时世界上最长的远洋航线。

自古以来，不同国家、不同文明沿着海上丝绸之路展开充分、深刻而广泛的交流，包括远洋船只的打造、海上航线的拓展、航海技术的演进、外贸港口的兴建、远洋货物的贩

Maritime Silk Road

Originating in the Qin (221-206 B.C.) and Han Dynasty (206 B.C.-A.D. 220) and thriving in the Tang (618-907) and Song Dynasty (960-1279), the Maritime Silk Road refers to the important sea routes linking China to the rest of the world. This mainly consists of two routes: the East China Sea Silk Route and the South China Sea Silk Route. The East China Sea Silk Route runs from China's Liaodong Peninsula and Jiaodong Peninsula to the Korean Peninsula, the Japanese Archipelago, and Southeast Asia. Alongside the continuous transportation of merchandise, Chinese culture was also transmitted overseas along the route, including elements like Confucianism, the legal system, Chinese characters, costumes, architecture, kung fu, and tea-drinking customs. The South China Sea Silk Route started from Guangzhou and Quanzhou and went to Southeast Asia and countries along the Indian Ocean. Beginning in the Han Dynasty, China expanded the Maritime Silk Road from east to west, while the Roman Empire sailed from west to east. The two finally met at the Indian Peninsula, thus extending the Maritime Silk Road to the Persian Gulf and the Red Sea. This was the first sea route across the Indian Ocean in world history and the longest ocean route at that time.

Through the ages, countries along the routes engaged in extensive and profound exchange with each other including building oceangoing vessels, expanding sea routes, improving navigation technology, constructing trade ports, transporting cargo, regulating foreign trade, managing the flow of immi-

运、对外贸易的管理、外来侨民的流动、官方使节的往来、音乐艺术的传播、异域物种的扩散等。海上丝绸之路成为中国与外国贸易往来和文化交流的海上大通道，推动了沿线各国的共同发展。2013年，中国提出共建“21世纪海上丝绸之路”重大倡议，让古丝绸之路焕发新的生机活力，推动亚欧非各国互利合作迈向新的历史高度。

grants, exchanging official envoys, disseminating music and art, and spreading exotic species. The Maritime Silk Road linked China with other countries by sea, promoted trade and cultural exchange, and contributed to the common development of countries along the routes. In 2013, China proposed the important initiative of the 21st Century Maritime Silk Road, injecting vigor and vitality into the ancient Silk Road and elevating mutually beneficial cooperation with countries in Asia, Europe and Africa to new heights.

茶马古道

茶马古道是古代中国西南和西北地区的商贸通道，以茶叶和马匹为主要交易内容，以马帮为主要运输工具。茶马古道以川藏道、滇藏道与青藏道为主，延伸出各条支线，构成了庞大的交通网络。茶叶从中国各地经藏区，通过喜马拉雅山口运往印度加尔各答，大量行销欧亚各国，茶马古道逐渐成为国际经贸和文化交流的大通道。第二次世界大战期间，世界各地通往中国战区的通道被切断，茶马古道成为运送各种物资的重要通道。茶马古道是人类历史上海拔最高、通行难度最大的高原文明古道，不仅是汉藏民族文化融合之路，也是中国各民族团结和睦之路。茶马古道是中国统一的多民族国家的历史见证，也是民族团结的重要象征。

Ancient Tea Horse Road

The Ancient Tea Horse Road refers to trade passages in southwestern and northwestern China in ancient times, which mainly traded tea and horses, using caravans primarily. The large transportation network offered three major routes, Sichuan-Tibet, Yunnan-Tibet, and Qinghai-Tibet route, as well as many branch routes. Tea from across China was transported to Tibet, then shipped to Kolkata, India, via the Himalayan passes, and sold in Europe and Asia on a massive scale, gradually making the Ancient Tea Horse Road an important channel for international trade and cultural exchange. As recently as WWII, it offered important access to China for the transportation of all kinds of supplies from the outside world when other transportation lines were cut off. The Road runs through plateau territory having the world's highest elevation and being the most difficult to traverse. It not only facilitated cultural integration between Han Chinese and Tibetans, but also contributed to the unity and harmony of China as multi-ethnic society.

四大发明

四大发明是中国古代四项具有世界影响力的科技发明，分别是造纸术、印刷术、指南针和火药。中国汉代的造纸术从8世纪开始便传入中亚、西亚和欧洲，为人类提供了经济、便利的书写材料，掀起一场人类文字载体革命。中国发明活字印刷术后，欧洲人也发明了活字印刷机，这些技术为书籍出版和普及奠定了基础，大大促进了文化传播，直接推动了欧洲文艺复兴和宗教改革。指南针和火药在13世纪传入欧洲，指南针为欧洲航海家的航海活动提供了技术条件，直接推动了大航海时代的开启；火药武器的使用改变了作战方式，加速了西欧封建时代的终结。

四大发明推动了中国古代的政治、经济、文化和社会发展，其经各种途径传至西方，为人类文明进步作出巨大贡献。

The Four Great Inventions of Ancient China

The four great inventions of ancient China refer to papermaking, printing, gunpowder, and the compass. They exerted far-reaching impact on the world. In the 8th century, Chinese papermaking technology, which was invented during the earlier Han Dynasty, was introduced to Central Asia, West Asia, and Europe, setting off a writing revolution by providing economical and convenient writing materials for humans. After the invention of printing by the Chinese, Europeans invented the movable-type printing press. These technologies paved the way for the publication and popularization of books, greatly facilitated cultural communication, and provided impetus for the Renaissance and the Reformation in Europe. The compass and gunpowder were introduced to Europe in the 13th century. The compass offered technical assistance to the European navigators, ushering in the Age of Discovery. Gunpowder weapons changed methods of warfare, accelerating the demise of the feudal system in Western Europe.

The four great inventions promoted political, economic, cultural, and social progress in ancient China. After they were introduced to the West through various channels, they contributed greatly to wider human advancement.

食物的交流

每一种食物都包含一部全球史，伴随着人类交往，各地食物的交流始终贯穿其中。中国是世界稻作的起源地，稻是中国古代最重要的粮食作物之一。从周朝起，中国稻谷北传朝鲜，南传菲律宾和印度尼西亚，成为这些地区的主要粮食之一。稻米和耕作技术传到日本后，逐渐成为其饮食和文化中的重要组成部分。

随着丝绸之路形成，各国交流活动增加，胡椒、葡萄、胡萝卜、辣椒等食材和香料进入中国，丰富了中国的饮食文化。新航路开辟后，美洲的特产马铃薯、玉米、番茄、甘薯、花生、南瓜和可可等也流向世界各地。16世纪，玉米进入中国，一度是皇家御用贡品，经18世纪推广后成为重要经济作物。明代后期，甘薯从东南亚传入中国，被大力推广用于赈灾。玉米和甘薯的引进，大大增加了粮食产量，直接导致古代中国人口增长，改变了中国的农作物种植结构。

民以食为天。食物的交流丰富了中国人的餐桌，促使中

Food's Global Spread

Each food has a history of spreading globally. A key conduit of people-to-people exchange is food. China is the origin of rice cultivation, and rice was one of the most important food crops in ancient China. During the Zhou Dynasty, China's rice started spreading northwards to the Korean peninsula and southwards to the Philippines and Indonesia, where it became cultivated as a major food crop. Rice and cultivation techniques also spread to Japan and gradually became central to its diet and culture.

As the Silk Road facilitated exchange between countries, black peppers, grapes, carrots, chili peppers, and other foods and spices arrived in China, enriching China's dietary culture. With the discovery of new sea routes to the East, potatoes, maize, tomatoes, sweet potatoes, peanuts, pumpkins, and cacao, among other items, spread from the Americas to other parts of the world. In the 16th century, maize was introduced to China and exalted as a tribute item to the imperial household. Large-scale cultivation in the 18th century made it an important cash crop, as it has been ever since. In the late Ming Dynasty, sweet potatoes traveled from Southeast Asia to China, where it was planted far and wide to fight famine. The introduction of maize and sweet potatoes led to an enormous hike in crop yield, which went on to feed a much larger population and change the mix of crops in ancient China.

Food is central to human survival. The arrival of foreign foods brought more flavors to the Chinese dining tables and

国饮食文化生机勃勃。中国美食与中国饮食文化传播到世界各地，并与当地饮食文化交流融通，推动了中外人文交流与民心相通。

enlivened Chinese dietary culture. Chinese foods and dietary culture also spread to other parts of the world and blended well with local foods and culture. Two-way spread promoted cultural exchange and fostered connectivity between Chinese and foreign peoples.

长安

长安，是陕西省西安市的古称。长安与罗马、开罗、雅典并称世界四大古都。长安是中国历史上建都朝代最多、建都时间最长、影响力最大的都城，是陆上丝绸之路的东方起点。在唐代，长安是东西方文化荟萃交流的集中地，是当时世界上最大的国际大都会。西域各国使臣、留学生、商人、僧侣、乐工、画师和舞蹈家在长安交往，来自不同族群、不同地域、不同国家的移民都侨居长安，来自波斯和罗马等异域的特色商品、服饰饮食、歌舞杂技、文化艺术、宗教信仰等都在长安交汇融通，来自印度、阿拉伯和拜占庭的天文学、医药学等科学技术也在长安传播，共同形成了“兼容并包、大气开放”的长安气象。大慈恩寺的大雁塔是古城长安的标志性建筑，大量历史文化遗产保留至今，见证着中外文化交流的辉煌历史。

Chang'an

Chang'an, today's Xi'an city in Shaanxi Province, is regarded as one of the world's "Four Great Ancient Capitals" alongside Rome, Cairo, and Athens. Historically, Chang'an served as capital for the longest period, straddling most dynasties, bestowing it unparalleled influence. It is the eastern terminus of the Silk Road. In the Tang Dynasty, Chang'an was the largest cosmopolitan city and facilitated the convergence and exchanges of oriental and occidental cultures. Envoys, international students, merchants, Buddhist monks, musicians, painters, and dancers from various countries mingled in Chang'an; people from different ethnic groups, regions, and countries lived in Chang'an; exotic commodities, costumes, food, songs and dances, acrobatics, culture, art, and religious beliefs from Persia, Rome and other foreign lands all converged in Chang'an; astronomy and medicine were disseminated from India, Arabia, and Byzantine to Chang'an. Together, they created a cosmopolitan atmosphere that was open and inclusive. Big Wild Goose Pagoda in Da Ci'en Temple, an iconic building in Chang'an, has been preserved alongside an abundance of Chang'an's historical and cultural heritage. They continue to bear witness to the glorious past of Sino-foreign cultural exchange.

上都

上都，位于内蒙古自治区锡林郭勒盟金莲川草原，始建于1259年，并于1263年由开平城改名上都。元上都作为元朝建立的第一个都城，在当时世界上具有举足轻重的地位，它大大地加强了中国与世界的联系，与影响和改变世界文明进程的许多重大历史事件及人类文明成果密切相关。13世纪，马可·波罗在上都觐见忽必烈，随后在《马可·波罗游记》中描绘了上都的繁华景象。几百年来，随着《马可·波罗游记》的广泛传播，上都的英文译名“Xanadu”在欧美国家传播甚广。

上都见证了元朝的辉煌历史，历经风雨洗礼，仍较完整地保留了原貌，成为目前保留最完整的草原都城。2012年，元上都遗址列入世界遗产名录。上都是古代文化融合的独特产物，既有游牧民族特征，又有汉文化和其他文化的特色，体现了多元文化的相互影响。

Shangdu (Xanadu)

Shangdu is located on the Jinlianchuan Grasslands of Xilingol League in Inner Mongolia Autonomous Region. It was built in 1259 and originally named Kaiping City, which was changed to Shangdu in 1263. As the first capital of the Yuan Dynasty, Shangdu was a prominent city that greatly boosted China's interactions with the rest of the world and featured prominently in many major historical events and civilizational milestones that shaped and changed the evolution of global civilizations. In the 13th century, Marco Polo met Kublai Khan in Shangdu. His book *Travels of Marco Polo* captured the hustle and bustle of the city, which he Romanized as "Xanadu." The wide dissemination of his writings over the hundreds of years since made "Xanadu" a ubiquitous word in Western countries.

A physical testimonial of the legendary history of the Yuan Dynasty, Shangdu remains mostly intact despite all the vicissitudes it endured, and it is considered the best-preserved grassland capital city in the world. In 2012, the Site of Xanadu was inscribed on the World Heritage List as a unique example of cultural fusion that demonstrates the coexistence and mutual assimilation of the nomadic people and the Han Chinese culture, among others.

泉州

泉州，是位于福建省的沿海城市。作为海上丝绸之路起点，泉州是古代商贸、文明和宗教交流的重要枢纽。在唐朝，泉州是中国对外贸易的四大口岸之一。宋元时期，泉州是中国的世界海洋商贸中心，是各国商旅云集、多元文化交融的“东方第一大港”，与100多个国家和地区通商贸易，呈现出“市井十洲人”“涨海声中万国商”的繁荣景象，被誉为“世界宗教博物馆”。

历史上，佛教、伊斯兰教、天主教、犹太教、基督新教、印度教、摩尼教等世界多种宗教在泉州广泛传播，留下了寺庙、教堂、遗址、石刻等大量文化遗产，共同见证了泉州多元文化汇集融合、多种宗教和谐共存的盛景。2021年，“泉州：宋元中国的世界海洋商贸中心”列入世界遗产名录。

Quanzhou

Quanzhou is a coastal city in Fujian Province. As the eastern terminus of the Maritime Silk Road, Quanzhou was an important hub of ancient commerce and trade, culture, and religious exchange. In the Tang Dynasty, Quanzhou was one of four major foreign trade ports in China. In the Song and Yuan dynasties, Quanzhou was China's hub for global maritime trade and reputed as "the largest port in the Orient." It was a magnet for merchants and travelers from all over the world and a melting pot of many cultures. The vibrancy of the bustling emporium that traded with over 100 countries and regions was captured by lines from poems such as "people from many foreign countries were a common sight on streets" and "when the tide rises, merchant ships from all countries come ashore to trade." It was dubbed a "World Museum of Religions."

Quanzhou was known as a "World Museum of Religions" for a long time. Historically, Buddhism, Islam, Catholicism, Judaism, Protectantism, Hinduism, Manichaeism, and other religions spread from other parts of the world and were widely observed in Quanzhou. They left behind a large volume of cultural heritage and historical sites such as temples, churches, and stone carvings, all physical testimony to a marvelous blend and assimilation of diverse cultures and the harmonious coexistence of different religions in Quanzhou. In 2021, "Quanzhou: Emporium of the World in Song-Yuan China" was inscribed on the World Heritage List.

广州

广州，濒临南海，素有中国“南大门”之称。作为海上丝绸之路的起点城市，广州一直是中国对外商贸的重要港口城市。唐宋时期，广州是世界著名的东方大港，开设了管理外贸事务的专门机构。明清时期，广州是东西方贸易往来和文化交流的唯一窗口，广州十三行作为清政府指定专营对外贸易的唯一合法机构，与亚洲、欧美主要国家都有直接贸易关系。西方的科技、工业、宗教和文化大多经由广州向中国传播。来自中国的器物、思想、文化等也通过广州走向世界。

自古以来，广州是广东乃至岭南区域政治、经济和文化中心。广州集散了来华的西方使臣、传教士、商人等，成为中国接纳西方文明的先行地和中外文化交流融合的枢纽。

Guangzhou

Located near the South China Sea, Guangzhou has long been known as the "southern gate of China." As the alternate terminus of the Maritime Silk Road, Guangzhou has always been an important port city for China's foreign trade. During the Tang and Song dynasties, Guangzhou was a world-renowned oriental port with a special agency tasked with managing foreign trade matters. During the Ming and Qing dynasties, Guangzhou was the only window for trade and cultural exchange between East and West. The thirteen trading houses ("the Thirteen Hongs in Canton"), the only legal institutions designated by the Qing government to specialize in foreign trade, developed direct trade relations with major countries in Asia, Europe, and the Americas. Guangzhou was the conduit for most Western technologies, industries, religions, and cultures to spread to China. Chinese artefacts, ideas, and culture also traveled from Guangzhou to other parts of the world.

Since ancient times, Guangzhou has been the political, economic, and cultural center of Guangdong and the wider Lingnan region (south of the Five Ridges). A gathering point for Western envoys, missionaries, and merchants to China, Guangzhou was a vanguard for welcoming Western civilizations and facilitating Sino-foreign cultural exchange and assimilation.

敦煌

敦煌，位于河西走廊最西端，地处甘肃、青海、新疆三省（区）交汇处，是古代中原通向西域的重要门户和丝绸之路的重要节点，也是古代中国最早对外开放的城市之一。古代中华文明同古印度、古希腊、古波斯文明在此汇聚交融，造就了独具特色的敦煌文化和开放包容的丝路精神。

敦煌地处丝路要道，各国使臣、将士、商贾、僧侣在此云集，丝绸、瓷器、珍宝、驼马、粮食等商品在此交易，形成了古代东西方贸易的中转站。敦煌是多种宗教和多民族文化的交汇地，西北古代少数民族在此交往交融，来自罗马、印度、阿拉伯等的世界文化在此融合荟萃，奠定了敦煌“华戎所交，一大都会”的历史地位，创造了多元和谐的敦煌文化，留下了美轮美奂的世界遗产——敦煌莫高窟。

Dunhuang

Dunhuang is located at the westernmost end of Hexi Corridor at the intersection of Gansu Province, Qinghai Province, and Xinjiang Uyghur Autonomous Region. In ancient times, it was an important gateway from the Central Plains to the Western Regions and an important node of the Silk Road. It was also one of the first cities to open to the outside world. The convergence and assimilation of the ancient Chinese civilization and ancient Indian, Greek, and Persian civilizations gave rise to unique Dunhuang culture and fostered the Silk Road spirit characterized by openness and inclusiveness.

As a critical node of the Silk Road, Dunhuang easily drew in envoys, military commanders and soldiers, merchants, and monks from all over the world. Silk, porcelain, jewelry, gems, camels, horses, and food, among other commodities, were conveniently traded in Dunhuang, making it a key transit point for ancient East-West trade. Many religions, ethnicities, and cultures came together in Dunhuang. Ethnic minorities in the northwest mingled and blended there, and foreign cultures from Rome, India, and Arab merged there. Historical records declared, "the coexistence of the Han people and the minorities made it no less important than a cosmopolitan city" and celebrated the pluralistic and harmonious Dunhuang culture and the splendid (now) World Heritage Mogao Caves.

张骞出使西域

公元前138年，西汉官员张骞奉汉武帝之命，率领一百多人第一次出使西域。他们西行进入河西走廊，不幸遭到匈奴扣留，经过长达十余年的留居终于寻机逃出，继续西行直至原定目的地。归途中，他们又遭匈奴扣押，后趁匈奴内乱逃回长安。张骞一行出使并停留西域十余年，详细了解了西域各国的政治经济状况、地理位置、风土人情，为汉朝开辟通往中亚的交通要道提供了宝贵资料。公元前119年，为联络乌孙等西域各国力量，张骞率使团再次出使西域，并促成乌孙国王与汉朝通使。在乌孙停留期间，张骞分别派遣副使到中亚、西亚、南亚广泛联络，相继吸引西域诸国使者来汉交流。

张骞肩负和平友好使命出使西域，一路艰难坎坷，备受辛劳，完成了卓有成效的外交旅行。他的两次出使，打破了

Zhang Qian's Diplomatic Missions to the Western Regions

In 138 B.C., Zhang Qian, an official in the Western Han Dynasty, was dispatched by Emperor Wu of Han on a diplomatic mission to the Western Regions with a delegation of over one hundred. While travelling westward through the Hexi Corridor, the envoy was captured by the Huns and detained for more than a decade before finally finding a chance to escape. They continued their journey westward to the intended destination. On their way back, they were detained by the Huns once again but escaped again when chaos among the Huns presented the opportunity to get back to Chang'an. During their decade-long stint in the Western Regions, Zhang Qian and members of the delegation documented in detail the political and economic status, geographic locations, folk customs, and cultures of the states there. This provided valuable information for the Han Dynasty to establish a thoroughfare to Central Asia. In 119 B.C., Zhang Qian was sent on a second diplomatic mission to make Wusun and other states in the Western Regions allies. He persuaded the King of Wusun to exchange envoys with Han. During his stay in Wusun, Zhang Qian sent deputies to Central, West, and South Asia. As a result of their painstaking efforts, many states in the Western Regions sent envoys to the Han imperial court.

Commissioned a task of peacemaking and friendship building, Zhang Qian completed his diplomatic journeys to great success against all odds. The two diplomatic missions erected a bridge between the Central Plains and the Western

中原和西域的隔绝状态，凿通了横贯东西的丝绸之路，促进了古代中国和西域各国的友好往来和文化传播，丰富了各国人民的文化生活，为人类文明进步作出重要贡献。

Regions and laid a foundation for the Silk Road across the East and West. He facilitated friendly exchange and cultural communication between ancient China and various states in the Western Regions and enriched the cultural activities of the peoples therein, making great contributions to the progress of human civilization.

郑和下西洋

1405年至1433年，中国航海家郑和率庞大船队七次出使，造访了东南亚、南亚、西亚、东非等地的三十多个国家和地区，拉开了15世纪世界“大航海”活动的序幕。尽管郑和船队是当时世界上最大的船队，但他们并没有侵占、掠夺，而是始终对沿线所有国家、民族以礼相待，友好交往。郑和使团不仅传递国家之间的友好问候，还帮当地人建造城池、驱逐海盗，传授造船、牛耕、畜牧、水稻种植、烹饪等先进技术。郑和第四次下西洋航行时，首次绕过阿拉伯半岛，抵达非洲，打通了中非之间的海路贸易。郑和带去的瓷器、丝绸、漆器等中国物产备受当地欢迎，一时间成为财富的象征。

郑和下西洋是中国古代规模最大、船只和海员最多、时间最久的海上远航活动，不仅缔造了世界航海业发展的里程碑，而且为发展中国和亚非各国的政治、文化、经济上的友好关系作出了卓越贡献，增进了各国人民对中国的了解，也

Zheng He's Voyages to the "Western Ocean"

From 1405 to 1433, Zheng He, a Chinese navigator, led a gigantic fleet on seven epic voyages to the "Western Ocean" (the Indian Ocean) and visited more than 30 countries and regions in Southeast Asia, South Asia, West Asia, and East Africa, which kicked off the Age of Discovery in the 15th century. At the time, Zheng He's fleet was unrivaled globally, but it never invaded or plundered anywhere. Instead, they communicated with all the countries and peoples along the way, treating them with courtesy and kindness. Zheng He's mission did more than convey friendly messages from China to other countries. It also helped local people build city walls and moats and fend off pirates as well as sharing advanced techniques such as shipbuilding, ox plowing, animal husbandry, rice planting, and cooking. On his fourth voyage, Zheng He passed the Arabian Peninsula and reached Africa for the first time, opening a sea trade route between China and Africa. His ships were loaded with Chinese porcelain, silk, and lacquerware, among others, which were immensely popular among the locals and became highly sought as symbols of wealth.

Zheng He's voyages to the "Western Ocean" were insurmountable in the history of ancient China in scale, number of ships, crew size, and duration. They were celebrated as milestones in world navigation history. They also helped forge friendly ties between China and Asian and African countries on political, cultural, and economic fronts. The expeditions helped others learn more about the Chinese people, and the Chinese

大大开阔了中国人的眼界，丰富了海外地理知识，建立了古代中国和亚非国家间的和平关系，使得海上丝绸之路得以畅通和绵延。

people greatly broadened their horizons and acquired more knowledge of world geography. The peaceful connections established between ancient China, Asia, and Africa by the voyages paved the way for the Maritime Silk Road to boom for a long time.

佛教传播

印度的佛教在两汉之际传入中国，至今已有2000多年的历史。从两汉经魏晋南北朝，再到隋唐，佛教逐步在中华大地上传播发展，并逐渐被中华文化吸收借鉴，成为中国本土化的佛教，即中国佛教。中国佛教以大乘佛教在中国的辉煌实践为标志，并与隋唐盛世交相辉映，使世界佛教的中心转移到了中国，进而影响到日本、韩国、越南、新加坡等国家。

为了将佛教传入中国，法显、玄奘等高僧历尽艰难，前往印度等地取经求法。龟兹（今新疆库车）高僧鸠摩罗什所译的经籍，有力推动了佛教传播和中国佛教思想发展。大规模的佛经汉译促使佛教进一步融入中国本土文化。唐代高僧鉴真受邀东渡日本，讲经诵法，推动了中日两国的友谊和文化交流，促进了佛教在东亚地区的传播。日本僧人空海也曾来到长安（今陕西西安）求学，带回大量中国佛教和书法经

Spread of Buddhism

Buddhism spread from India to China during the Han Dynasty, and since has been practiced in China for over two millennia. From the Han Dynasty to the Wei, Jin, Southern, and Northern Dynasties, and then Sui and Tang dynasties, Indian Buddhism gradually spread and evolved on Chinese soil, assimilated into the Chinese culture over time, and eventually took hold as Chinese Buddhism. Mahayana Buddhism, the dominant form of Chinese Buddhism, peaked in the prosperous and booming Sui and Tang dynasties, which shifted the center of Buddhism from India to China and propelled the spread of Buddhism further to Japan, Korea, Vietnam, and Singapore.

With an aim to introduce Buddhism to China, Faxian, Xuanzang, and other Buddhist monks made pilgrimages to India and beyond in seek of Buddhist scriptures and doctrines. The scriptures and books translated by Kumarajiva, a Buddhist monk from the Kingdom of Kucha (present-day Kuqa County, Xinjiang), significantly facilitated the spread of Buddhism and shaped the doctrines of Chinese Buddhism. Large-scale translation of Buddhist scriptures into the Chinese language further boosted the assimilation of Buddhism into Chinese culture. Jianzhen, an eminent Buddhist monk in the Tang Dynasty, was invited by Japan to visit and sailed there to preach about Buddhist scriptures and doctrines. He promoted friendship and cultural exchange between China and Japan and propagated Buddhism in East Asia. Japanese Buddhist monk Kukai once studied in Chang'an (present-day Xi'an, Shaanxi Province) and

典，推进了日本佛教的发展。

佛教的传播体现了思想文化传播的双向特性，在这个过程中，佛教深深影响了中国传统文化，并逐渐发展成为世界性的宗教。

brought many Chinese Buddhist scriptures and classic calligraphy works back to Japan, promoting Buddhism there.

The spread of Buddhism remains living proof of the omni-directional nature of philosophical and cultural dissemination. After its arrival in China, Buddhism exerted a huge impact on traditional Chinese culture and gradually became a world religion.

基督教传播

基督教于635年开始传入中国，当时被中国人称为景教，经两百余年的广泛传播后，一度被封建统治者禁止。元朝时期，基督教（景教和罗马公教）再次传入中国，但随着元朝灭亡又转入沉寂。直到16世纪，葡萄牙传教士开始进入中国传教。明代末期，意大利籍传教士罗明坚（Michele Ruggieri）、利玛窦（Matteo Ricci）来华传教，定居广东。利玛窦等人与以徐光启、李之藻等人为代表的儒家文人和士大夫广泛结交，借助中国儒家经典对天主教进行再阐释，为不同文化之间的对话提供了有益契机，天主教由此在中国获得广泛传播。1807年，英国伦敦教会派遣马礼逊来华传教，他翻译并刻印了第一部完整的汉语版《圣经》，发展了华人传教士并将美国传教士引入中国，推动了基督新教在中国沿海地区传播。

基督教在中国的传播，不仅引介了西方宗教、人文思想、科学技术，还推动"东学西渐"，为18世纪启蒙运动提供丰富思想资源，推进了人类文明发展进程。

Spread of Christianity

Christianity spread to China in 635, where it was called *Jingjiao* (the Luminous Religion) by Chinese people. It swept across the country for over two hundred years before being banned by imperial rulers. During the Yuan Dynasty, Christianity (Jingjiao and Catholicism) was brought back to China but fell into oblivion after the Yuan Dynasty was overthrown. Such obscurity carried over until the 16th century when Portuguese missionaries arrived to preach in China. Towards the end of the Ming Dynasty, Italian missionaries Michele Ruggieri and Matteo Ricci settled in Guangdong to evangelize there. Ricci and his fellow evangelists hobnobbed with Confucian scholars and government officials represented by Xu Guangqi and Li Zhizao. They adapted interpretations of Catholicism to Confucianism, which created conduits for dialogue between the two cultures. Thus began a sweeping propagation of Catholicism in China. In 1807, Robert Morrison was sent by the London Missionary Society to preach in China. He was the first to translate and print the entire Bible in the Chinese language, convert Chinese people into missionaries, and bring in missionaries from the United States of America. His work facilitated the spread of Protestantism in the coastal areas of China.

The spread of Christianity not only brought Western religious beliefs, cultures, philosophy, science, and technology, but also kindled the "Westward Spread of Eastern Learning," fueling the Enlightenment in the 18th century with complementary Eastern wisdom and helping advance human civilization.

“伊儒会通”

自明清始，一批精通伊斯兰文化且熟谙中华文化的中国穆斯林学者开展了以著译为标志的“伊儒会通”活动，对伊斯兰文化进行汉语翻译和编撰，以期将外来伊斯兰文化与儒家文化为主体的本土文化相会通。其主要代表人物是王岱舆、马注、刘智、马德新等，代表作品有《正教真诠》《清真大学》《希真正答》《天方性理》《天方典礼》《天方至圣实录》《清真指南》和《大化总归》等。

“伊儒会通”既是伊斯兰教在中国生根发展的现实需要，也是基于中国穆斯林知识分子对中华文化的强烈认同。其核心精神在于引导不同文明及其载体之间的交往交流交融，体现了中华文明兼收并蓄的基本态度，对促进伊斯兰教中国化产生了深远的影响。

Convergence of Islam and Confucianism

In the Ming (1368-1644) and Qing (1616-1911) dynasties, a group of Chinese Muslim scholars who were well-versed in both Islamic and Chinese cultures began fostering the confluence of Islam and Confucianism. These initiatives facilitated the convergence of Islamic culture and Confucianism by producing translation and compilations of Islamic teachings in Chinese. Key figures included Wang Daiyu, Ma Zhu, Liu Zhi, Ma Dexin, and others. Well-known works included *A True Explanation of the Right Religion* (*Zhengjiao Zhenquan*), *The Great Learning of Islam* (*Qingzhen Daxue*), *Rare and True Answers* (*Xizhen Zhengda*) , *The Natures and Principles of Islam* (*Tianfang Xingli*), *The Rites of Islam* (*Tianfang Dianli*), *The Real Record of the Last Prophet of Islam* (*Tianfang Zhisheng Shilu*), *The Compass of Islam* (*Qingzhen Zhinan*), and *Final Destiny of the Universe* (*Dahua Zonggui*).

Practically speaking, so many Chinese Muslim intellectuals strongly identifying with Chinese culture ensured the convergence of Islam and Confucianism and helped Islam take root in China. The situation created a conducive atmosphere for civilizations and their elements to flow and mingle with one another. These gains testified to the openness and inclusiveness of Chinese civilization towards others and exerted far-reaching influence on the Sinicization of Islam.

遣隋遣唐使

600年，为了加强与中国的交往，日本开始向中国派出遣隋使。学习中国佛法和文化制度是派出遣隋使的主要目的。日本曾多次派出遣隋使，为日后大规模派遣遣唐使做好了各方面的准备。

7—9世纪，日本先后向唐朝派出十几次遣唐使团。遣唐使团的构成和规模因时期而不同，每次派遣多达百人以上，有时多达五百余人。遣唐使的派遣目的在于向中国学习。许多律令制度、文化艺术、科学技术、风俗习惯等通过遣唐使传入日本，对日本的社会发展产生了重大影响。

在遣隋遣唐使前往中国长达几百年的学习中，他们不仅将隋唐时期的礼仪、法制、文化带回日本，也让隋唐人民了解到邻邦日本的文化与历史发展，成为中日友好交流史上浓墨重彩的一笔。

Japanese Missions to Sui-Tang China

To increase its contact with China, Japan started to dispatch official envoys to the Sui Dynasty in 600 who were mainly tasked with learning about Chinese Buddhism, culture, and governance. The many missions to Sui China prepared Japan for larger missions to Tang China in every way.

During the 7th and 9th centuries, Japan sent a dozen missions to Tang China on different occasions. Group composition and size varied, but they were invariably large, always exceeding 100 and sometimes over 500 individuals. Tasked with learning from China, the missions brought back myriad laws, bureaucratic practices, culture, art, science, technology, and folk customs which, shaped Japanese society in substantial ways.

The centuries of Japanese missions to Sui-Tang China not only introduced rituals, laws, and culture of Sui-Tang China to Japan but also offered the Sui-Tang Chinese a glimpse of the culture and history of their neighbor Japan, making it a profound event in the history of Sino-Japan friendly exchange.

汉字的传播

汉字是汉语的载体，是中国文化的独特形式，是记录华夏文明的“活化石”。作为世界上最古老的文字之一，汉字已有6000年左右的历史。汉字不仅为中国人所使用，而且传入与中国邻近的朝鲜、越南和日本并远播海外，推动和促进了中外文化交流。从汉字的流传及使用的历史来看，到了隋唐时期，东亚地区已开始形成一个以汉字为标志的、在文化上有共同特色的区域，即“汉字文化圈”。

汉字的西传则相对要晚得多。明清之际来华传教士首先向欧洲介绍汉字。中国汉字的西传及对汉语语法的介绍，一方面满足了欧洲学者对于东方语言的兴趣，另一方面，传教士所提供的汉语词典及语法文献，直接促使西方语言学家从比较语言学的角度对中国语言开展研究，直至今日仍方兴未艾。

The Popularity of Chinese Characters

Chinese characters are a key medium for communication in the Chinese language. They are also unique carriers of Chinese culture and "living fossils" of Chinese civilization. With nearly 6000 years of history, Chinese characters are one of the world's oldest scripts, and their users are not limited to Chinese people and include those in neighboring Korea, Vietnam, Japan, and beyond. Chinese characters promote cultural exchange between China and the rest of the world. In the Sui (581-618) and Tang (618-907) dynasties, a sphere with a shared cultural identity marked by Chinese characters, known as the "Chinese Character Culture Circle" gradually took shape.

The westward spread of Chinese characters only happened much later. Missionaries first introduced them to Europe during the Ming (1368-1644) and Qing (1616-1911) dynasties. The introduction of the characters and grammar of the Chinese language satisfied a thirst for Oriental languages among European scholars. Missionaries compiled dictionaries and researched Chinese grammar to make it more available to Western linguists seeking to undertake comparative linguistic analyses of the Chinese language, which has continued unabated until this day.

礼法制度传播

作为中国古代文化的重要组成部分，法律制度伴随着中国政治、经济、文化的演进而不断发展，形成了独特风格。经过儒家伦理道德观念与国家法律长达数百年的相互渗透和融合，秦汉时期形成了中国古代特有的礼法传统。隋唐时期，各国使节将中国的礼法制度引介到本国。明清时期，来华的传教士在向西方社会介绍中国的国情、历史、文化的同时，也重点引介了中国的礼法制度，为启蒙时代的欧洲展示了一个理想型的政府。伏尔泰、莱布尼茨、孟德斯鸠、魁奈等启蒙思想家广泛讨论并赞赏中国的礼法制度，兴起了“欧洲中国热”的历史现象。中国古代礼法制度的传播为亚欧国家建立更加合理完善的政治制度提供了参照与借鉴。

Dissemination of Rituals and Laws

An important component of the ancient Chinese culture, the Chinese legal system evolved alongside political, economic, and cultural changes and stood out due to its uniqueness. With the mutual influence and fusion of the Confucian moral values and code and laws of the state over several hundred years, the system of rituals and laws unique to ancient China took hold in the Qin and Han dynasties. During Sui-Tang China, foreign envoys introduced China's rituals and laws to their country. When explaining China's specifics, history, and culture to Western society, missionaries that visited China during the Ming and Qing dynasties highlighted the system of rituals and laws that they perceived as a good form of government upon returning to Europe in the Age of Enlightenment. The Chinese system of rituals and laws was widely discussed and praised by Enlightenment thinkers such as Voltaire, Leibniz, Montesquieu, and Quesnay. All this culminated in the phenomenal Chinoiserie. The spread of the ancient Chinese system of rituals and laws provided reference for Asian and European states to establish a more reasonable and sound political system.

中医药传播

中医药是中华优秀传统文化和中国古代科技的杰出代表，其在几千年的医学实践中不断发展、壮大，是中国人民的智慧结晶。唐宋时期，有关中医的信息通过阿拉伯世界传入欧洲，为欧洲医药的发展注入东方元素。特别是在唐代，由于中国文化的高度繁荣和巨大影响，吸引各国使节、商人、学者来华学习。他们不但将中国制度、文化、语言和文字引入本国，而且将中华民族的各种发明创造，包括医药学说都带回了本国。今天日本的“汉方”和韩国的“四象医学”，就是在中医基础上发展而来的典型代表。

明末清初之际，欧洲传教士来华传教，同时也将中医和中药知识带回欧洲。波兰传教士卜弥格是中医西传的开拓者，他率先向西方介绍《黄帝内经》《脉经》，撰写中医学术著作，开启了西方对中医的研究，推动了中草药的西传，有利于中医药传播并造福各国人民。

Popularization of Traditional Chinese Medicine

Traditional Chinese medicine is the quintessence of fine traditional Chinese culture and scientific and technological progress in ancient China. Refined over thousands of years of medical practice, it is the perfect representative of Chinese wisdom. During the Tang and Song dynasties, knowledge of Chinese medicine spread to Europe via the Arab world and heavily influenced European medicine. The spread of the Chinese medicine was particularly active in the Tang Dynasty when the hugely vibrant and influential culture attracted many envoys, merchants, and scholars from other countries. When they returned home, they brought not only systems, culture, language, and written characters, but also various creations and inventions of the Chinese people including medical theories and practices. Japanese Kampo and the Korean Sasang Constitutional Medicine are typical examples of foreign medicines with roots in traditional Chinese medicine.

From the late Ming Dynasty to early Qing Dynasty, European missionaries came to China to preach and brought Chinese medicine and knowledge about it back to Europe. Michel Boym, a Polish Jesuit missionary, was a pioneer in introducing Chinese medicine to the West. He wrote about *Yellow Emperor's Internal Canon of Medicine* (*Huangdi Neijing*) and *Canon of Pulse* (*Maijing*) and authored a treatise on the Chinese medicine. He also launched the study of the Chinese medicine in the West and propelled the Westward spread of Chinese herbal medicines, extending their benefits to people in more countries.

表演艺术传播

中国表演艺术历史悠久，其对外传播主要分为境内传播和境外传播。境内传播主要通过“乐宴来使”等方式，让国外文化使者充分认识和了解中国表演艺术，并将其吸收、引进到自己国家。境外传播主要通过“外派使臣”等方式，由国内文化使者将中国表演艺术直接传播到其他国家和地区。中国的舞蹈、音乐也受印度、波斯、中亚的影响，异域艺术为中国乐舞注入了新的美感，发挥长久而特殊的功能，如乐器琵琶、舞蹈敦煌舞，至今为中国民众喜爱。

近代以来，中国表演艺术大规模向海外传播，具有鲜明中国文化特色的地方戏曲、传统歌舞、武术表演、杂技表演等形式多样、内容丰富的表演艺术活动不断走上国际舞台，给不同国家和地区的人民带来美妙的艺术享受，打开了世界了解中国的新窗口，促进了中外表演艺术的交流互鉴。

Performing Arts Communication

Across China's long history of performing arts, they have been disseminated through two major channels: the domestic arena and overseas arena. Domestically, "les banquets for envoys," among other forms, have been organized for foreign cultural envoys in hopes that they can appreciate Chinese performing arts more deeply and absorb and introduce them back home. Overseas communication is mainly realized by "sending envoys abroad" to perform Chinese arts. Chinese dance and music are also subject to influences from India, Persia, and Central Asia. Performing arts of foreign origins have brought new aesthetic values to Chinese music and dance forms. Their profound and unique impacts can be seen in the musical instrument Pipa and Dunhuang Dance, which continue to be popular among Chinese people.

In modern times, Chinese performing arts have spread abroad on a larger scale. Local operas, traditional music and dances, martial arts, acrobatics, and other performing arts with distinctive Chinese cultural characteristics have constantly landed on the international stage, bringing profound enjoyment of rich artistic content to people in different countries and regions. A new window for the world to understand China was lifted open, and exchange and mutual learning of Chinese and foreign performing arts gained momentum.

《马可·波罗游记》

意大利人马可·波罗是中西文明交流史中的重要人物。1271年，17岁的马可·波罗随父辈从中亚的陆上丝绸之路抵达元大都（今北京），并在中国生活了17年。马可·波罗依据在中国和亚洲各国的游历见闻，口述了周游东方的故事，由鲁斯蒂谦记录并写成《马可·波罗游记》。游记重点记述了忽必烈统治时期元朝各地的物产市集、风土人情、奇闻轶事等，还记录了日本、东南亚、印度等地的情况。

《马可·波罗游记》是第一部全面、深入介绍中国的游记，是西方认识中国历程中里程碑性的著作，掀起了历史上第一次西方"中国热"。作为中西文化交流的先驱，马可·波罗和《马可·波罗游记》一直为后人所追随，为中世纪的欧洲带去了希望，也对日后新航路的开辟产生了巨大影响。

Travels of Marco Polo

Venetian Marco Polo remains a prominent figure in the history of exchange between the Chinese and Western civilizations. In 1271, 17-year-old Marco Polo and his parents traveled along the Silk Road in Central Asia to Dadu of Yuan (present-day Beijing). He ended up staying in China for 17 years. Marco Polo gave oral accounts of his travels in China and some other Asian countries, which Rustichello da Pisa documented and compiled into the *Travels of Marco Polo*. The book focused on local products, fairs, folk customs, and anecdotes experienced in places he traveled during the rule of Kublai Khan. They also contained accounts of Japan, Southeast Asia, and India.

The *Travels of Marco Polo* was the first travelogue to offer a comprehensive and in-depth account of China. A milestone work in terms of informing the West about China, it set off the first wave of "Chinoiserie." As a vanguard of cultural exchange between China and the West, Marco Polo became an esteemed figure, and the travelogue became highly sought-after among later generations. The book brought hope to Medieval Europe and catalyzed the discovery of new sea routes to the East.

“东学西渐”

中西方文明交流源远流长。16至18世纪，中西方文明开始了持续的、多方面的交往和相互影响，即“西学东渐”“东学西渐”。“东学西渐”，就是中国的学术思想、礼法制度、文化艺术、科学技术等传入西方。

来华的西方传教士成为当时“东学西渐”的主要承担者。他们通过翻译中国古代典籍，撰写有关中国的文章和书籍，将中国思想文化引介到西方。例如，16世纪利玛窦用拉丁文翻译朱熹《四书》，17世纪末数十种中国经典译本在欧洲流行，同时，欧洲学者研究中国哲学文化的著作不断涌现。他们努力了解中国社会，在寄往欧洲的书信和报告中热情洋溢地介绍中国的地理、社会、民生。在他们的记述中，中国地大物博、国力雄厚，政治制度优越，人民安乐富足，是拥有强大的理性文明而备受艳羡的东方大国。

传教士们的记述激发了欧洲知识分子了解中国甚至崇尚中国理性文明的强烈渴望，引发了启蒙思想界关于中国的高

"Westward Spread of Eastern Learning"

Chinese and Western civilizations have enjoyed a long history of exchange which culminated in the 16th to 18th centuries when interactions and mutual influence became continuous on multiple fronts. They were characterized as "Eastward Spread of Western Learning" and "Westward Spread of Eastern Learning," the latter referring to the introduction of China's academic thought, system of rituals and laws, culture and art, and science and technology to the West.

Western missionaries who visited China acted as the main conduit of the "Westward Spread of Eastern Learning." They spread Chinese philosophies and culture to the West by translating Chinese classics and writing articles and books on China. For example, Matteo Ricci translated the *Four Books* compiled by scholar Zhu Xi into Latin. By the end of the 17th century, translations of scores of Chinese classics were circulating in Europe. Meanwhile, European scholars started publishing more writings about Chinese philosophies and culture. Those visiting China went out of their way to learn as much about it as possible. They wrote and sent to Europe glowing letters and reports on China's geography, society, and people. They portrayed China as an oriental power enviable for its vastness, abundance, prosperity, superior political system, happy and affluent people, and preeminent but rational civilization.

The accounts of the missionaries aroused a strong desire among European intellectuals to understand China and many even developed reverence for the rational civilization of Chi-

度关注和广泛讨论，乃至“中国热”在欧洲的蓬勃兴起。一个有着辽阔国土、悠久历史、灿烂文化的中国正式进入欧洲人的视野，推动欧洲思想史的发展进程，为欧洲中世纪末期的社会变革提供了重要条件，展现出这一文明交流活动的世界性意义。

na, prompting Enlightenment figures to engage in animated and extensive discussions about the country, eventually giving rise to sensational "Chinoiserie." China, a country with a vast territory, long history, and splendid culture, officially arrived in the headspace of Europeans. The "Westward Spread of Eastern Learning" catalyzed intellectual progress and provided important favorable conditions for social changes towards the end of the Middle Ages in Europe. Such developments speak volumes to the global significance of this wave of civilizational exchange.

“西学东渐”

16世纪，西方传教士来华，揭开了“西学东渐”的序幕，西方学术、宗教等在中国本土的传播引起很大反响。西方文化的传入与中国近代思想文化自身的变迁相互交融，推动中华文明在兼收并蓄中历久弥新。

西方传教士在中国传教的同时，也将西方的自然、社会、人文知识带入中国。他们参与绘制了中国历史上第一张世界地图《坤舆万国全图》，展现了世界上不同国家和地区，开创了中国绘制世界地图的先例。他们翻译的西方学术经典，促进了中国传统文化和传统科学的发展。当时，徐光启、李之藻、方以智等中国开明的知识分子受“西学”影响，为中国文化注入西方知识，推动了中西方文化交融。1607年，利玛窦和徐光启译成古希腊数学经典著作《几何原本》前六卷，书中大量数学名词对中国数学思想和数学方法的发展产生了积极影响。到了中华民国时期，“西学东渐”进入新的时期，“西学”传播内容更加丰富。这一时期，关于西方政治、哲学、经济、法学等内容的西学书籍被大量翻译，对中国的学术、思想、政治和社会经济都产生了重要影响。

"Eastward Spread of Western Learning"

In the 16th century, Western missionaries started arriving in China, setting the stage for "Eastward Spread of Western Learning." The spread of Western knowledge and religions was sensational in China. Fusion of Western cultures and evolving Chinese philosophies and cultures in modern times kept Chinese civilization vibrant and relevant.

While preaching, the Western missionaries also disseminated knowledge about nature, society, and culture. They helped draw *Map of the Ten Thousand Countries of the Earth* (*Kunyu Wanguo Quantu*), the first world map in China to show other countries and regions in the world, which set precedent for global cartography in China. Translated Western classics fueled progress of traditional culture and science and technology in China. At the time, enlightened Chinese intellectuals exposed to "Western Learning" such as Xu Guangqi, Li Zhizao, and Fang Yizhi adopted and applied Western knowledge and facilitated a fusion of Chinese and Western cultures. In 1607, Matteo Ricci and Xu Guangqi translated the first six volumes of *Elements*, the ancient Greek mathematical treatise, into Chinese, introducing considerable mathematics jargons to the country that went on to exert a major impact on mathematical thinking and methodologies in China. In the Republic of China, the "Eastward Spread of Western Learning" advanced to a new stage, marked by a wider range of "Western Learning" being introduced. During this stage, many Western books on politics, philosophy, economics, law, and other disciplines were translated, exerting a substantial impact on academic, ideological, political, and socio-economic fronts.

马克思主义经典翻译传播

马克思主义在中国的早期传播，离不开译者先驱的不懈努力。马克思主义经典文献，主要包括马克思、恩格斯、列宁的著作以及斯大林的部分重要著作。19世纪末，马克思、恩格斯的名字和马克思主义著作的文字片段开始传入中国。马克思主义经典翻译传播在新文化运动时期达到高峰。1920年8月，陈望道翻译的《共产党宣言》全译本在上海出版，这是中国历史上第一部完整的中文版马克思主义经典著作，为中国共产党的创立奠定了重要的思想基础和理论基础。由此，中国无产阶级革命知识分子和马克思主义理论家、翻译家开始大量翻译马克思主义经典著作，有力促进了民族解放和振兴。马克思主义经典在中国的翻译、传播已经有120余年，推动马克思主义基本原理同中国具体实际相结合、同中华优秀传统文化相结合，为中国革命、建设、改革提供了强大思想武器。

马克思主义经典在世界上的广泛传播，指导和推动了不同时期国际工人运动的联合和斗争。在马克思主义影响下，马克思主义政党在世界范围内如雨后春笋般建立和发展起来，推动了一大批社会主义国家的诞生，极大推进了人类文明进程。

Translation and Dissemination of Marxist Classics

The early spread of Marxism in China would not have been successful without the relentless work of pioneering translators. Key Marxist classics by Marx, Engels, Lenin, and some important works of Stalin were all translated and printed in China. By the end of the 19th century, Marx and Engels were already known in China through excerpts of their classic works. The pinnacle for translation of Marxist classics arrived during the New Culture Movement. In August 1920, a full translation of the *Communist Manifesto* by Chen Wangdao was published in Shanghai. The first of its kind in China, this complete Chinese version of a classic Marxist work formed an ideological and theoretical ground for the founding of the Communist Party of China. Ever since, Chinese proletarian revolutionary intellectuals, Marxist theorists, and translators have been translating Marxist classics in large volumes, which effectively fomented national liberation and revitalization. Translation and dissemination of Marxist classics in China has continued for more than 120 years. Relevant to China's national reality and easily aligned with excellent traditional Chinese culture, the basic principles of Marxism provided a powerful ideological weapon for China's revolution, construction, and reform.

During a handful of widespread international labor movements, Marxist classics served as guidance and helped unite workers in their struggles. Answering the call of Marxism, Marxist political parties mushroomed around the world and founded numerous socialist countries, greatly advancing human civilization.

亚洲经典著作互译计划

2019年5月15日，习近平在亚洲文明对话大会上提出，中国愿同有关国家一道，实施亚洲经典著作互译计划和亚洲影视交流合作计划，帮助人们加深对彼此文化的理解和欣赏，为展示和传播文明之美打造交流互鉴平台。

亚洲经典著作互译计划是以翻译推动亚洲文明交流互鉴的重要倡议与合作机制，重点推进亚洲47国的文化互译和文明互鉴，其秘书处设在北京语言大学。截至2022年10月，中国已与新加坡、巴基斯坦、韩国、伊朗、老挝、亚美尼亚、吉尔吉斯斯坦、阿塞拜疆、蒙古国等签署了经典著作互译出版备忘录，为展示和传播亚洲各国文明之美、共建亚洲命运共同体作出积极贡献。

Translation Program for Asian Classics

On May 15, 2019, Xi Jinping announced at the Conference on Dialogue of Asian Civilizations that China would be happy to launch initiatives with relevant countries to translate Asian classics both from and into Chinese and promote film and TV exchange and cooperation in Asia. The intention was to help people in Asia better understand and appreciate each other's cultures and build a platform for exchange and mutual learning that would empower the best of Asian civilizations to spread and become known to more people around the world.

The Translation Program for Asian Classics from and into Chinese became a major initiative and cooperation mechanism to promote mutual understanding and appreciation of Asian civilizations through translation works amongst 47 Asian countries. The Program's secretariat works out of Beijing Language and Culture University. As of October 2022, China had signed memoranda of understanding on translation and publication of classic works with Singapore, Pakistan, Republic of Korea, Iran, Laos, Armenia, Kyrgyzstan, Azerbaijan, and Mongolia, contributing to the promotion and spread of the best of Asian civilization and fostering a community with a shared future for all Asians.

当代中国与世界文明互鉴

Mutual Learning between Contemporary Chinese and World Civilizations

人类社会创造的各种文明，都闪烁着璀璨光芒。多样性是人类文明的魅力所在，更是世界发展的活力之源。当代中国秉持平等、互鉴、对话、包容的文明观，倡导弘扬全人类共同价值，同国际社会一道，努力开创世界各国人文交流、文化交融、民心相通新局面，推动文明交流互鉴，促进人类文明进步。

All civilizations created by human society are highly valuable. Diversity adds to the charm of human civilization and is the source of vitality of world development. Today, China upholds the principles of equality, mutual learning, dialogue, and inclusiveness and advocates promoting the common values of humanity. China stands ready to work together with the international community to open new avenues for enhanced exchange and understanding among different peoples and better interaction and integration of diversified cultures by promoting exchange and mutual learning among civilizations for human progress.

创造人类文明新形态

人类文明新形态是习近平从文明视角对中国共产党百年历史辉煌和中国式现代化新道路的伟大成就所作出的总结和概括。2021年7月1日，习近平在庆祝中国共产党成立一百周年的大会上提出，中国坚持和发展中国特色社会主义，推动物质文明、政治文明、精神文明、社会文明、生态文明协调发展，创造了中国式现代化新道路，创造了人类文明新形态。

数千年来，中华民族走着一条不同于其他国家和民族的文明发展道路。在漫长的历史进程中，中华民族形成了讲仁爱、重民本、守诚信、崇正义、尚和合、求大同的精神特质和发展形态。中国式现代化深深植根于中华优秀传统文化，体现科学社会主义的先进本质，借鉴吸收一切人类优秀文明成果，代表人类文明进步的发展方向，展现了不同于西方现代化模式的新图景，是一种全新的人类文明形态。中国式现代化所创造的人类文明新形态，破解了人类社会发展的诸多难题，为广大发展中国家独立自主迈向现代化树立了典范，为人类对更好社会制度的探索提供了中国方案。

A New Model for Human Advancement

"A new model for human advancement" is the phrase President Xi Jinping used to summarize the glorious history of the CPC and the great achievements along the new Chinese path to modernization from the perspective of civilization. "China has upheld and developed socialism with Chinese characteristics and driven coordinated progress in material, political, cultural-ethical, social, and ecological terms," he said on July 1, 2021, at a ceremony marking the centenary of the CPC. "We have pioneered a new and uniquely Chinese path to modernization and created a new model for human advancement."

For thousands of years, the Chinese nation has followed a path of civilizational development distinct from other countries and nations. Along the long historical process, the Chinese nation formed spiritual characteristics and development patterns underscoring benevolence, the importance of all people, integrity, justice, harmony, and unity. The Chinese path to modernization is deeply rooted in the best of traditional Chinese culture. It reflects the advanced nature of scientific socialism and draws on all the most outstanding achievements of human civilization. It represents the development direction of human civilization, offers a new vision that contrasts the Western modernization model, and produces a new model for human advancement. This new model created by the Chinese path to modernization has solved many problems hindering the development of human society, set an example for other developing countries to move towards modernization independently, and provided Chinese solutions for mankind to explore better social systems.

坚持胸怀天下

“必须坚持胸怀天下”是中共二十大报告对习近平新时代中国特色社会主义思想世界观和方法论的高度凝练，充分彰显中国共产党人的天下胸怀与世界担当。天下观是中国古老的世界观与秩序观。在传统天下观中，自我与他者的区别是开化与未开化之别。因此，中华文明在处理自身与外部世界关系时，秉持文化高于种族、天下高于国家的基本理念，把天下大同作为终极理想。这就决定了中国的天下观具有非常强的包容性、开放性、多元性与兼容性。

中国共产党人继承传统天下观的文明包容性、多样性、开放性精神，把传统天下体系的经验和智慧创造性地转化为“全球治理”的中国方案，在国际秩序建构上坚持求同存异、和而不同、协和万邦、世界大同的理念，积极回应各国人民普遍关切，努力为解决人类面临的共同问题贡献中国智慧和中国力量。

Maintain Global Vision

"We must maintain global vision," read a sentence in the report to the 20th CPC National Congress, providing a succinct summary of the world outlook and methodology of Xi Jinping Thought on Socialism with Chinese Characteristics for a New Era. The sentence highlights the global vision and sense of global responsibility of Communist China. It has roots in the ancient Chinese view of the world and order of things. In the traditional Chinese worldview, the difference between self and others was similar to civilized and uncivilized. Therefore, when navigating relations between itself and the outside world, Chinese civilization adheres to the basic prioritization of culture over race and sees the world as above the country, rating global harmony as the loftiest ideal. This makes China's world outlook very inclusive, open, diverse, and tolerant.

Chinese communists have creatively transformed traditional experiences and wisdom into Chinese solutions for improving global governance. They advocate "seeking common ground while setting aside differences," "harmony without uniformity," "harmony among all nations," and "great unity of the world" when building the world order. They actively respond to the common concerns of the people of all countries and strive to contribute Chinese wisdom and strength to resolving the various problems facing humankind.

尊重世界文明多样性

尊重世界文明多样性的理念深深植根于中华文明的精神谱系之中。中国文化注重以和为贵，中华文明强调追求多样性的和谐，强调以和合的精神尊重容纳多样性与差异性。“和”是事物生成变化的必要条件，不同事物间调和、融合才能生成繁盛的、新的事物。“和谐”并不要求抹平差异性，而是坚持和而不同。

正是由于强调和谐和合的文化精神，中国人并不以冲突的眼光来看待国家间关系。习近平指出：“不同国家、民族的思想文化各有千秋，只有姹紫嫣红之别，而无高低优劣之分。”中国本着尊重多元、包容差异、兼容并包的原则，在平等相待与相互尊重的基础上与各国打交道，共同维护世界和平稳定，促进人类文明进步。

Respect Diversity of Civilizations

The principle of respecting the diversity of world civilizations is deeply rooted in Chinese civilization. Chinese culture values harmony, while Chinese civilization emphasizes "harmony without uniformity" and respect for diversity and differences. Harmony is essential for the birth and growth of things. Only by harmonizing and integrating different things can we kindle booming new things. Harmony can only be achieved by maintaining differences rather than setting them aside.

Chinese culture values harmonious coexistence, and Chinese people do not consider conflict between countries inevitable. "Civilizations only vary from each other, and no civilization is superior to others," said President Xi Jinping. Based on the principles of respecting diversity and accommodating differences, China works with all countries based on equality and mutual respect to jointly safeguard world peace and stability and promote the progress of human civilization.

借鉴吸收人类一切优秀文明成果

中华文明尊重远客，重视比较，努力汲取众家之长。儒家经典《论语》首章即强调学而知之的重要性。《论语》中还强调“三人行，必有我师焉”“见贤思齐”，这些古语都在强调学习他人长处的重要性。

历史上，中华文明曾经学习、消化、吸纳外来佛教文明，形成本土化的中国化佛教诸流派，佛教又与本土的儒、道教融合，形成了理学，后传到东亚，成为东亚文化圈的精神文明。16世纪中叶，利玛窦等传教士来华，传播天主教与西方文化，中国又开始了400多年学习西方文化的历程。

中华文明善于博采众长，借鉴吸纳其他文明的长处与精华，融会贯通，自成一体，由此铸就了中华文明的辉煌灿烂。当代中国秉持兼收并蓄、开放包容的理念，以海纳百川的宽阔胸襟借鉴吸收人类一切优秀文明成果，深化人类文明交流互鉴，推动建设更加美好的世界。

Draw on the Achievements of Other Civilizations

Chinese civilization respects guests from afar and attaches importance to comparing oneself with others and learning from their strengths. The first chapter of *The Analects of Confucius* emphasizes the importance of learning and understanding. The book stresses the importance of drawing from the strengths of others with axioms such as "When three people walk together, at least one teacher is always available" and "When we see a man of virtue and talent, we should emulate him." These old sayings underscore the importance of learning from others' strengths.

Historically, Chinese civilization learned, digested, and absorbed many concepts of Buddhism, a foreign religion, to form various schools of localized Chinese Buddhism. Buddhism merged with local Confucianism and Daoism to produce Neo-Confucianism, which later spread to East Asian neighbors and gained dominant influence in the East Asian cultural circle. In the middle of the 16th century, Matteo Ricci and other missionaries ventured to China to spread Catholicism and Western culture. China began to learn from Western culture, an endeavor that has continued for more than 400 years since.

The Chinese civilization excels at drawing on the strengths and essence of other civilizations and integrating them into a whole to create a more brilliant Chinese civilization. Contemporary China, following the principles of inclusiveness and openness, learns from all the outstanding achievements of human civilization like a vast ocean welcoming all rivers, and deepens exchanges and mutual learning among human civilizations to promote the construction of a better world.

弘扬全人类共同价值

2015年9月28日，习近平在第七十届联合国大会一般性辩论上指出：“‘大道之行也，天下为公。’和平、发展、公平、正义、民主、自由，是全人类的共同价值，也是联合国的崇高目标。”

和平与发展是人类的共同事业，也是当今时代的主题，关乎所有人的生存权和发展权。公平与正义是人类的共同理想，也是国际秩序的基石。民主与自由是人类的共同追求，是各国人民共同的权利。全人类共同价值是构建人类命运共同体的价值内核和理念指引，是解答“世界之问”的中国主张和中国智慧。它虽然是由中国率先提出，但并非仅是中国的发明创造，而是顺应时代发展潮流、契合各国人民期待的价值追求；它既是对西方价值观的吸收、超越，也是对中华优秀传统文化的继承、创新与弘扬，旨在以人类共同利益为交汇点，凝聚不同文明的价值共识，增进不同文明的交流互鉴。

Promote the Common Values of Mankind

President Xi Jinping addressed the high-level general debate of the 70th session of the United Nations General Assembly on September 28, 2015. "As an ancient Chinese adage goes, 'The greatest ideal is to create a world truly shared by all,'" he said there. "Peace, development, fairness, justice, democracy, and freedom are common values of all mankind and the lofty goals of the United Nations."

Peace and development are the common aspirations of mankind and the theme of the current era. Global consensus supports the rights to subsistence and development of all people. Fairness and justice are common ideals of mankind and the cornerstone of the international order. Democracy and freedom are the common goals of mankind and the common rights of all peoples. The common values of mankind are the core values and guiding principles for building a global community of shared future, which represent China's solutions to tackling the pressing problems facing today's world. Although these values were first proposed by China, they are not an invention of China, but rather objectives that conform to the development trends of the times and represent the aspirations of people from all countries. They drew upon Western values and have since transcended them by inheriting fine traditional Chinese culture and transforming them to suit new circumstances. They aim to center the shared interests of mankind as the common ground, build consensus among different civilizations, and promote exchange and mutual learning.

推动构建人类命运共同体

人类命运共同体的理念包含“天下太平”“共享大同”的世界建设愿景、“怀柔远人”“协和万邦”的国家相处之道、“和为贵”“言而有信”的交往准则、“计利当计天下利”的义利观、“己欲立而立人，己欲达而达人”的仁爱精神、“先天下之忧而忧，后天下之乐而乐”的使命担当以及“海纳百川，有容乃大”的宽广胸怀。推动构建人类命运共同体，不是以一种制度代替另一种制度，不是以一种文明代替另一种文明，而是不同社会制度、不同意识形态、不同历史文化、不同发展水平的国家在国际事务中利益共生、权利共享、责任共担。

构建人类命运共同体是世界各国人民前途所在。中国倡导国际社会从伙伴关系、安全格局、经济发展、文明交流、生态建设等方面作出努力，建设持久和平、普遍安全、共同繁荣、开放包容、清洁美丽的世界。

Promote Construction of a Global Community of Shared Future

The concept of a global community of shared future reflects a vision of building the world into a peaceful and harmonious place and promoting principles for handling international relations such as "winning over distant people with kindness" and "peaceful coexistence among all nations," as well as codes of concord such as "harmony is most precious" and "always keep one's word." It also hearkens to principles of pursuing the greater good and shared interests as expressed in the lines such as "Considering the gains to the world when calculating one's own gains," "To establish oneself, first let others establish themselves; and to achieve one's own goals, first let others achieve theirs," and "Be the first to worry about troubles and the last to enjoy pleasure." It connotes the broadminded nature of "a vast ocean that admits all rivers." Promoting construction of a global community of shared future does not involve replacing one system with another or one civilization with another. It is about promoting mutually beneficial coexistence by sharing benefits and responsibilities among countries regardless of social systems, ideological beliefs, historical and cultural backgrounds, or levels of development.

A global community of shared future is the inevitable future of people all over the world. China believes that the international community should devote more effort to building partnerships and promoting security, economic development, cultural exchange, and ecological progress to foster a planet of lasting peace, universal security, and common prosperity and a home that is open, inclusive, and clean and beautiful.

文明交流互鉴

习近平指出：“文明是多彩的，人类文明因多样才有交流互鉴的价值。”世界基于不同历史、国情、习俗等因素孕育出不同文明，各有独特魅力和深厚底蕴，中国始终秉持平等、谦虚的态度了解各种文明的真谛。习近平曾做过这样一个比喻：“正如中国人喜欢茶而比利时人喜爱啤酒一样，茶的含蓄内敛和酒的热烈奔放代表了品味生命、解读世界的两种不同方式。但是，茶和酒并不是不可兼容的，既可以酒逢知己千杯少，也可以品茶品味品人生。”

文明的多样性决定了文明交流互鉴的必然性。交流互鉴是文明发展的本质要求。中华文明正是在同世界文明的交流互鉴中不断博采众长，发展壮大。在承认世界文明多样性的基础上，中国提出了文明交流互鉴的基本原则，倡导不同文明要取长补短、共同进步，让文明交流互鉴成为推动人类社会进步的动力、维护世界和平的纽带。

Exchange and Mutual Learning between Civilizations

"Civilizations have come in different colors, and this diversity has made exchange and mutual learning among civilizations relevant and valuable," said President Xi. Contrasting histories, national conditions, and customs globally have birthed different civilizations, each possessing unique charm and heritage of unmatched depth. China considers all civilizations equal and has modestly sought to understand other civilizations. President Xi once illustrated the diversity with a metaphor: "The Chinese people are fond of tea and Belgians love beer. To me, the moderate tea drinker and passionate beer lover represent two ways of understanding life and knowing the world, and I find them equally rewarding. When good friends get together, they may want to drink to their hearts' content to show their friendship. They may also choose to sit down quietly and drink tea while chatting about their lives."

Diversity of civilizations demands exchange and mutual learning among them because they are essential to development. Through exchange and learning, the Chinese civilization continues to draw on the strengths of others and grow stronger. While embracing diversity, China has presented basic principles for exchange and mutual learning among civilizations that advocate different civilizations learning from each other and making progress together—to utilize exchange among civilizations as a source of inspiration for advancing all of human society and bonds that maintain world peace.

增强中华文明传播力影响力

增强中华文明传播力影响力是指要向世界讲好中国故事、传播好中国声音，展现可信、可爱、可敬的中国形象，推动中华文化更好走向世界。“可信”展示的是中国的公信力，“可爱”展示的是中国的温润度，“可敬”展示的是中国的责任感，这些都是中华文明数千年沉淀的文化特质。一诺千金背后的“可信”、人伦和合背后的“可爱”、大同理想背后的“可敬”，是中华文明不间断传承的重要原因。

中国将坚守中华文化立场，坚持创造性转化、创新性发展，在世界舞台上讲好中国故事、传播好中国声音，展现中华文明的悠久历史和人文底蕴，促使世界读懂中国。

Strengthen International Communication Capabilities

By strengthening our international communication capabilities, we will be better able to tell China's stories, make China's voice heard, and showcase a nation that is credible, appealing, and respectable—more accurately depicting China to the world. That China is credible, appealing, and respectable means that it is trustworthy, friendly, and highly responsible, all cultural traits that have been formulated over thousands of years of Chinese civilization. China is credible because it treasures the virtue of keeping promises, it is appealing because it features harmonious relationships between people, and it is respectable because it strives for the common good. These are important reasons Chinese civilization has persisted.

China will firmly uphold Chinese culture and develop it creatively, tell China's stories well, make China's voice heard, highlight its long history and rich heritage, and help the world understand China.

万物并育而不相害，道并行而不相悖

“万物并育而不相害，道并行而不相悖”，出自儒家经典《礼记·中庸》，意思是：万物竞相生长繁育，但是彼此之间并不妨害；日月运行、四时更替各有各的规律，但相互之间不冲突。这是中国古人通过对自然万物和谐共生的观察而总结出的规律性认识，体现了“和而不同”“天人合一”的思想。这种思想不同于西方的“多元主义”，它强调多元之间的相互依存、平衡与共生，而非斗争、冲突和妥协。在中国人看来，文明是包容的，只要秉持包容精神，就不存在所谓“文明冲突”，就可以实现文明和谐。

中国秉持“万物并育而不相害，道并行而不相悖”理念，倡导各国和睦相处、合作共赢，共同建设一个持久和平、普遍安全、共同繁荣、开放包容、清洁美丽的世界。

All Living Things Can Be Nourished without Injuring One Another, and All Roads Can Run Parallel without Overrunning Each Other

This sentence from the Confucian classic *The Book of Rites* means that all things grow and breed in competition, but do not harm each other. The movement of the sun, the moon, and the shift between the four seasons each follow their own rules, so they do not conflict with each other. This understanding, kindled by ancient Chinese people through their observations of the harmonious coexistence of all things in nature, embodies the idea of "harmony without uniformity" and "harmony between humanity and nature." Contrasting the "pluralism" of the West, the philosophy of ancient Chinese people emphasizes interdependence, balance, and coexistence among various parties instead of fighting, conflict, and compromise. In the eyes of the Chinese people, civilization is inclusive. If the spirit of inclusiveness is upheld, the so-called "clash of civilizations" can be avoided, and harmony among civilizations can be achieved.

Cherishing the idea that "all living things can be nourished without injuring one another, and all roads can run parallel without overrunning each other," China champions harmonious coexistence and win-win cooperation among countries to jointly build a world of lasting peace, universal security, common prosperity, openness, inclusiveness, welcoming, and beautiful.

平等、互鉴、对话、包容的文明观

平等、互鉴、对话、包容的文明观，展现了中华文明“天下为公”的博大情怀和“美美与共”的远见卓识。中共十八大以来，习近平深刻把握“人类文明多样性是世界的基本特征，也是人类进步的源泉”的基本规律，提出“文明因交流而多彩，文明因互鉴而丰富”的重要论断，倡导弘扬平等、互鉴、对话、包容的文明观，弘扬中华文明蕴含的全人类共同价值，推动构建人类命运共同体。

人类社会发展史是一部多元文明共生并进的历史。文明的繁盛、人类的进步，离不开求同存异、开放包容，离不开文明交流、互学互鉴。中国秉持平等、互鉴、对话、包容的文明观，愿同各国一道，坚持和而不同，倡导美美与共，为人类文明进步作出更大贡献。

Equality, Mutual Learning, Dialogue, and Inclusiveness among Civilizations

The Chinese nation's fondness for equality, mutual learning, dialogue, and inclusiveness among civilizations reinforces its lofty ideal of pursuing the common good and farsighted vision in appreciating diversity. President Xi Jinping deeply understands that "Diversity of human civilizations not only defines our world, but also drives progress of mankind," and since the 18th CPC National Congress, he has been stressing that "Civilizations become richer and more colorful through exchange and mutual learning" and advocating equality, mutual learning, dialogue and inclusiveness among civilizations. He has promoted the common values of humankind, which are also embodied in Chinese civilization, to promote construction of a global community of shared future.

The history of social development is one of coexistence and parallel progress among various civilizations. The ability to seek common ground while setting aside differences, practice openness and inclusiveness, and conduct exchange and mutual learning are vital to the prosperity of civilization and human progress. China upholds equality, mutual learning, dialogue, and inclusiveness and wants to work with other countries to promote harmony while respecting diversity to jointly make greater contributions to the progress of human civilization.

以文明交流超越文明隔阂、文明互鉴超越文明冲突、文明共存超越文明优越

文明因多样而交流，因交流而互鉴，因互鉴而发展。不同文明、制度、道路的交流互鉴可以为人类社会进步提供强大动力。世界上有200多个国家和地区、2500多个民族、70多亿人口，文化的差异不应该成为交流的障碍，更不能成为对抗的理由。加强人文交往是各国人民的共同愿望，符合各国共同利益。

中国反对文化霸权，主张尊重世界文明多样性，以交流促理解，以互鉴促团结，以共存促发展，推动共建人类命运共同体。国际社会只有抵制文明歧视、打破文明隔阂、反对文明冲突，让人类创造的各种文明交相辉映，编织出斑斓绚丽的图画，才能让各种文明和谐共存，让人人享有文化滋养。

Exchange not Estrangement, Mutual Learning over Cultural Clashes, and Equality Instead of Superiority

Diversity spurs interaction among civilizations, which in turn promotes mutual learning and further development. Exchange and mutual learning among different civilizations with distinct systems and paths can provide a strong impetus for the progress of human society. The world is home to more than 200 countries and regions, more than 2,500 ethnic groups, and a population of more than 7 billion. Cultural differences should not impede communication or be a reason for confrontation. Strengthening people-to-people and cultural exchange is the common aspiration of the people of all countries that corresponds with the common interests of all countries.

China opposes cultural hegemony and advocates respecting diversity in world civilizations and promoting understanding through exchange, unity through mutual learning, and development through coexistence to continue construction of a global community of shared future. Only when the international community opposes discrimination against any civilization, works to break down the barriers between civilizations, prohibits conflicts between civilizations, and empowers various human civilizations to add splendor to each other and create symphonies together can all civilizations coexist harmoniously and ensure everyone enjoys cultural nourishment.

各美其美，美人之美，美美与共，天下大同

“各美其美，美人之美，美美与共，天下大同”是20世纪90年代初中国社会学家费孝通先生提出的文化设想，阐明了文化的“交流”“互鉴”与“共存”这一根本价值诉求。“各美其美”是指各个民族、国家要弘扬自己的优秀文化。“美人之美”是指要学习别人的优秀文化。“美美与共，天下大同”则是说，各个民族、国家的优秀文化要互相包容、互相尊重，多元文化互相融合，形成一个多彩的世界，不同文明和而不同、兼收并蓄，进而实现大同。

中华文明拥有5000多年悠久历史，开放包容一直是其特色之一。从西汉时张骞出使西域，到明代郑和七次远洋航海，再到今天的“一带一路”等，中华文明都在为亚洲乃至世界文明作出自己的贡献。“各美其美，美人之美，美美与共，天下大同”，是中华文明为人类文明进步贡献的中国智慧。

All Civilizations Can Appreciate Each Other's Beauty While Valuing Their Own and Achieve Common Development

This fundamental principle for cultural exchange, mutual learning, and healthy coexistence was outlined by Chinese sociologist Fei Xiaotong in the early 1990s. He suggested that each nation and country carry forward its own excellent culture, learn from others' excellent culture, and tolerate and respect each other so that diverse cultures will interact with each other to form a colorful and harmonious world.

Chinese civilization has a long history of more than 5,000 years, and openness and inclusiveness have always been among its characteristics. From Zhang Qian's mission to the Western Regions in the Western Han Dynasty (206 B.C.-A.D. 25) and Zheng He's seven ocean voyages in the Ming Dynasty (1368-1644) to the Belt and Road Initiative of today, Chinese civilization has always made key contributions to Asian and world civilizations. The saying "All civilizations can appreciate each other's beauty while valuing their own and achieve common development" embodies the Chinese wisdom and represents Chinese civilization's contribution to the progress of human civilization.

全球文明倡议

在各国前途命运紧密相连的今天，不同文明包容共存、交流互鉴，在推动人类社会现代化进程、繁荣世界文明百花园中具有不可替代的作用。2023年3月，习近平在中国共产党与世界政党高层对话会上提出“全球文明倡议”，表达了中国共产党愿同各国政党一道，推进具有本国特色的现代化事业、促进全球文明交流互鉴、推动构建人类命运共同体的真诚愿望。

全球文明倡议以四个“共同倡导”为核心内涵，即共同倡导尊重世界文明多样性、共同倡导弘扬全人类共同价值、共同倡导重视文明传承和创新、共同倡导加强国际人文交流合作。这一倡议秉持平等、互鉴、对话、包容的文明观，倡导弘扬全人类共同价值，主张以文明交流超越文明隔阂、文明互鉴超越文明冲突、文明包容超越文明优越，推动各国优秀传统文化在现代化进程中实现创造性转化、创新性发展，

Global Civilization Initiative (GCI)

The futures of all countries are now closely connected, so tolerance, coexistence, exchange and mutual learning among different civilizations have been playing an even more important role in advancing modernization and enabling human civilizations to thrive. In March 2023, Xi Jinping introduced the "Global Civilization Initiative" at the CPC in Dialogue with World Political Parties High-Level Meeting, expressing the sincere desire of the Communist Party of China to work with political parties in other countries to promote the modernization cause with national characteristics, promote exchange and mutual learning among all civilizations, and promote the construction of a global community of shared future.

The Global Civilization Initiative focuses on "common advocates": joint advocacy for respect for the diversity of civilizations, advocacy for the common values of humanity, advocacy for the importance of inheritance and innovation of civilizations, and advocacy for robust international people-to-people exchanges and cooperation. GCI upholds the principles of equality, mutual learning, dialogue, and inclusiveness and promotes the common values of humanity. Cultural exchange must overpower estrangement, mutual learning must come before clashes, and coexistence must overcome feelings of superiority. Countries should be encouraged to push for creative transformation and innovative development of their fine traditional cultures and promote mutual understanding and friendship among people of all countries to jointly advance the

促进各国人民相知相亲，共同推动人类文明发展进步。

全球文明倡议是继全球发展倡议、全球安全倡议后，新时代中国为国际社会提供的又一重要公共产品，为推动世界现代化进程、促进人类文明进步提供了中国方案。

progress of human civilizations.

The Global Civilization Initiative is another important public product China is providing to the international community in the new era, following the Global Development Initiative and the Global Security Initiative. It offers Chinese solutions that promote world modernization and forward progress of human civilization.

全方位对外开放

开放是当代中国的鲜明标识，是国家繁荣发展的必由之路。改革开放以来，中国坚持对外开放基本国策，不断拓展对外开放的广度和深度，实现了从封闭半封闭到全方位开放的历史性转变，也实现了中国同世界关系的历史性变革。1979年，中共中央、国务院决定对广东、福建两省的对外经济活动实行特殊政策和灵活措施，并于1980年在深圳、珠海、汕头、厦门创办经济特区，标志着中国对外开放正式启程。20世纪80年代中期至90年代初，对外开放的范围由特区逐步扩大到沿海、沿江、沿边和内陆地区，形成了从沿海到内地、由南向北、自东向西区域梯次开放的格局。2001年，中国加入世界贸易组织，区域性对外开放逐渐转变为全方位对外开放。

中共十八大以来，中国实行更加积极主动的开放战略，推动形成更大范围、更宽领域、更深层次的对外开放格局，不断以中国新发展为世界提供新机遇，推动建设开放型世界经济，更好惠及各国人民。中国将以更加开放的姿态拥抱世界、以更有活力的文明成就贡献世界，同世界各国携手建设美好世界。

Opening Up on All Fronts

Opening up is a distinctive characteristic of contemporary China and the path the country must take to achieve prosperity and development. Since the late 1970s, China has maintained opening up as a basic national policy and continued expanding its scope and depth. The country has undergone a historic change from being closed or semi-closed to opening to the outside world on all fronts, a historic change in its relations with the world. In 1979, the CPC Central Committee and the State Council decided to implement special policies and flexible measures for foreign-related economic activities in Guangdong and Fujian provinces. In 1980, special economic zones were established in Shenzhen, Zhuhai, Shantou, and Xiamen, marking the official commencement of China's opening up. From the mid-1980s to the early 1990s, the scope of opening gradually expanded from special economic zones to some coastal areas and then from coast to inland, from south to north, and from east to west, to cover some riverside, border, and inland areas. In 2001, China acceded into the World Trade Organization, which further expanded opening up from certain regions to all fronts.

Since the 18th CPC National Congress, China has implemented a more proactive strategy to promote opening up on a larger scale, across more areas and in greater depth, constantly providing new opportunities for the world through its development and bringing more benefits to the people of all countries by promoting an open world economy. China will continue to open wider to the world, contribute to the world with a more vibrant civilization, and work together with other countries to build a better world.

“一带一路”

“一带一路”是“丝绸之路经济带”和“21世纪海上丝绸之路”的简称。2013年9月和10月，习近平在出访中亚和东南亚国家期间，先后提出共建“丝绸之路经济带”和“21世纪海上丝绸之路”的重大倡议，得到国际社会高度关注。

“一带一路”秉持共商、共建、共享原则，以政策沟通、设施联通、贸易畅通、资金融通、民心相通为主要内容，致力于与沿线各国全方位推进务实合作，打造政治互信、经济融合、文化包容的利益共同体、命运共同体、责任共同体。“一带一路”国际合作高峰论坛是这一倡议框架下最高规格的国际活动。

“一带一路”将和平与发展置于国际合作的核心，符合有关各方共同利益，顺应地区和全球合作潮流，成为深受欢迎的国际公共产品和国际合作平台，涵盖世界上三分之二的国家和三分之一的国际组织。截至2023年2月，中国已与151个国家、32个国际组织签署200余份“一带一路”合作

The Belt and Road Initiative

"Belt and Road" is the short form of the Silk Road Economic Belt and the 21st Century Maritime Silk Road. During his visit to Central Asia in September 2013 and to Southeast Asia in October of the same year, President Xi Jinping respectively proposed jointly building the Silk Road Economic Belt and the 21st Century Maritime Silk Road, which received major attention from the international community.

Upholding the principles of extensive consultation, joint contributions, and shared benefits, the Belt and Road focuses on promoting policy coordination, infrastructure connectivity, unimpeded trade, financial integration, and people-to-people bonds. It is committed to comprehensively promoting pragmatic cooperation among participating countries and building a community with shared interests, future, and responsibility featuring political mutual trust, economic integration, and cultural inclusion. The Belt and Road Forum for International Cooperation is the highest-standard international activity under the framework of this initiative.

The Belt and Road Initiative positions peace and development at the core of international cooperation, which aligns with the common interests of all parties and conforms to the trends of regional and global cooperation. It has become a popular international public good and international cooperation platform involving two thirds of countries and one third of international organizations in the world. As of February 2023, China had signed more than 200 Belt and Road cooperation documents

文件，形成3000多个合作项目，投资规模近1万亿美元。“一带一路”国际合作有力促进了共建国家的经济社会发展和人民相知相亲，为当地人民带来了实实在在的获得感。

with 151 countries and more than 32 international organizations, formulating more than 3,000 cooperation projects with an investment scale of nearly US$1 trillion. International cooperation under the Belt and Road Initiative has effectively promoted the economic and social development of participating countries and people-to-people bonds by bringing a real sense of fulfilment to affected local people.

北京冬奥会、冬残奥会

第24届冬季奥林匹克运动会、第13届冬季残疾人奥林匹克运动会分别于2022年2月4日至2月20日、2022年3月4日至3月13日在北京举办。这是继2008年夏季奥运会之后，北京第二次举办奥运会。两场赛事盛会、三个冬奥赛区、四场开闭幕式精彩纷呈，人类命运共同体的主题贯穿始终，中华文化和冰雪元素交相辉映，体现了自然之美、人文之美、运动之美。北京携手张家口向世界奉献了一届简约、安全、精彩的奥运盛会，全面兑现了对国际社会的庄严承诺，北京成为世界上首座“双奥之城”。

比赛期间，来自世界各地的体育健儿在赛场上相互尊重、彼此激励、突破极限，在激情的比赛中完美演绎了“更快、更高、更强——更团结”的奥林匹克格言和“勇气、决心、激励、平等”的残奥价值观。北京冬奥会、冬残奥会的成功举办，促进了不同文明交流互鉴，为推动全球团结合作、共克时艰发挥了重要作用，也为动荡不安的世界带来了信心和希望，向世界发出了“一起向未来”的时代强音。

Beijing Olympic Winter Games and Paralympic Games

The 24th Olympic Winter Games and the 13th Paralympic Winter Games were held in Beijing from February 4 to 20, 2022, and from March 4 to 13, 2022, respectively. It was Beijing's second hosting of the Olympic Games after the 2008 Summer Olympics. The Beijing 2022 Games were held in three Winter Olympic competition zones, bookended by splendid opening and closing ceremonies. The theme of a global community of shared future flavored the whole process. Chinese cultural elements and ice and snow elements complemented each other to express the beauty of nature, humanity, and sports. Together with Zhangjiakou City, Beijing successfully hosted a simple, safe, and wonderful Olympic Games for the world, fulfilling its solemn commitment to the international community while becoming the world's first city to host both Winter and Summer Olympics.

During the competition, athletes from all over the world demonstrated respect, encouraged each other, and pushed their limits. Throughout the fierce competition, they perfectly captured the Olympic motto of "faster, higher, stronger—together" and the Paralympic values of "courage, determination, inspiration, and equality." The successful hosting of the Beijing Olympic Winter Games and the Paralympic Winter Games promoted exchange and mutual learning among different civilizations, played an important role in promoting global solidarity and cooperation to overcome difficulties, and brought confidence and hope to a volatile world, sending a strong signal for the world to venture "together into the future."

中国国际服务贸易交易会

随着经济全球化深入推进，服务贸易日益成为国际贸易的重要组成部分和各国经贸合作的重要领域，为世界经济增长注入了新动能。中国致力于促进更高水平对外开放，积极同各国深化服务贸易投资合作，自2012年起举办中国国际服务贸易交易会，为服务贸易搭建国家级、国际性、综合型大规模展会和交易平台。

中国国际服务贸易交易会（服贸会）、中国进出口商品交易会（广交会）、中国国际进口博览会（进博会）是中国对外开放的三大最高级别展会平台。多年来，中国通过服贸会等国际性贸易平台与各国互通有无，共享中国市场红利，以开放促合作，以互利促共赢。

China International Fair for Trade in Services (CIFTIS)

Advancement of economic globalization has made trade in services an increasingly important part of international trade and an important area for economic and trade cooperation among countries—injecting new impetus into world economic growth. China is committed to promoting a higher level of openness to the outside world and actively deepening investment cooperation in service trade with other countries. China has held the CIFTIS since 2012 to build a national-level, comprehensive, large-scale exhibition and trading platform for the world's service trade.

The CIFTIS, the China Import and Export Fair (Guangzhou Fair), and the China International Import Expo (CIIE) are the three highest level exhibition platforms in China to promote opening up. Over the years, China has exchanged as needed with other countries through international trade platforms such as the CIFTIS, sharing Chinese market's growth dividends and promoting win-win cooperation through openness.

博鳌亚洲论坛

博鳌亚洲论坛是一个总部设在中国的国际组织，由29个成员国共同发起，于2001年2月正式成立，其初衷是促进亚洲经济一体化。论坛每年定期在海南博鳌举行年会，旨在为政府、企业及专家学者提供一个共商经济、社会、环境等相关问题的高层对话平台。

目前，论坛已成为亚洲以及其他大洲有关国家政府、工商界和学术界领袖就亚洲以及全球重要事务进行对话的高层次平台。论坛立足亚洲，面向世界，坚持以经济发展为主线，同时积极向科技创新、健康、教育、文化、媒体等领域拓展，为亚洲及世界的和平、繁荣与可持续发展贡献力量。

Boao Forum for Asia

The Boao Forum for Asia is an international organization headquartered in China which now welcomes participation from 29 member countries after its formal establishment in February 2001. Its purpose is to promote economic integration in Asia. The forum regularly holds its annual meeting in Boao, Hainan Province, and aims to provide a high-level dialogue platform for governments, enterprises, experts, and scholars to discuss economic, social, environmental, and other related issues.

Now, the forum has become a high-level platform for representatives of governments, businesses, and academia from relevant countries in Asia and other continents to conduct dialogue on important issues related to Asia and the world. The forum, based in Asia and oriented towards the world, focuses on economic development and has been actively expanding to cover fields such as scientific and technological innovation, health, education, culture, and media to contribute to peace, prosperity, and sustainable development in Asia and the world.

亚洲文明对话大会

2019年5月，亚洲文明对话大会在北京举行。来自亚洲全部47个国家和世界其他国家及国际组织的1300余位会议代表共同出席大会。大会聚焦“亚洲文明交流互鉴与命运共同体”主题，在开幕式、平行分论坛、亚洲文化嘉年华、亚洲文明周等四大板块共110余场文明交流活动中，共商亚洲文明发展之道，共话亚洲合作共赢大计，达成广泛共识并发表《亚洲文明对话大会2019北京共识》，形成了四大类26项推动文明交流互鉴的务实举措和合作成果。

习近平出席亚洲文明对话大会开幕式，并发表题为《深化文明交流互鉴，共建亚洲命运共同体》的主旨演讲，提出了加强文明交流互鉴的四点主张，即坚持相互尊重、平等相待，坚持美人之美、美美与共，坚持开放包容、互学互鉴，坚持与时俱进、创新发展，为夯实共建亚洲命运共同体、人类命运共同体的人文基础提供了中国方案。

The Conference on Dialogue of Asian Civilizations (CDAC)

In May 2019, the CDAC was held in Beijing. More than 1,300 representatives from all 47 countries in Asia and other countries and international organizations attended the conference. Themed "exchange and mutual learning among Asian civilizations as well as a community with a shared future," the conference featured more than 110 activities including an opening ceremony, sub-forums, Asian cultural carnival, and Asian civilization week. Participants discussed the development of Asian civilizations and win-win cooperation among Asian countries, reached broad consensus, and released the 2019 Beijing Consensus of the Conference on Dialogue of Asian Civilizations. It included 26 practical measures and cooperation outcomes in four major categories to promote exchange and mutual learning among civilizations.

President Xi attended the opening ceremony of the CDAC and delivered a keynote speech titled "Deepening Exchange and Mutual Learning Among Civilizations for an Asian Community with a Shared Future," in which he made the following proposals: to respect each other and treat each other as equals, to appreciate the culture and values of others as one does one's own, to stay open and inclusive and draw on each other's strengths, and to advance with the times and explore new ground in development. These compose a Chinese solution that would lay a solid cultural foundation for building a community of shared future in Asia and in the rest of the world.

中国—阿拉伯国家峰会

2022年12月，首届中国—阿拉伯国家峰会在沙特首都利雅得举行，习近平和20多位阿盟成员国领导人、国际组织负责人出席峰会。习近平在峰会上发表主旨讲话，回顾中阿双方源远流长的友好交往史，提炼跨越千年、历久弥坚的中阿友好精神，指出守望相助是中阿友好的鲜明特征，平等互利是中阿友好的不竭动力，包容互鉴是中阿友好的价值取向。习近平提出支持发展、粮食安全、卫生健康、绿色创新、能源安全、文明对话、青年成才、安全稳定等中阿务实合作"八大共同行动"，为构建更加紧密的中阿命运共同体规划了前进路径。中阿峰会还发表了《首届中阿峰会利雅得宣言》《中阿全面合作规划纲要》《深化面向和平与发展的中阿战略伙伴关系文件》三份成果文件，明确将全力构建面向新时代的中阿命运共同体作为中国和阿拉伯国家的共同意愿、目标、行动。

中国和阿拉伯国家人口约占世界人口总数的四分之一，

China-Arab States Summit

In December 2022, the first China-Arab States Summit was held in Riyadh, capital of Saudi Arabia. Chinese President Xi Jinping and more than 20 leaders of League of Arab States member countries and heads of international organizations attended. Xi delivered a keynote speech reviewing the long history of friendly exchange between China and Arab countries and elaborating on the China-Arab friendship that has strengthened over thousands of years. He said that solidarity and mutual assistance are distinct features of the China-Arab friendship, equality and mutual benefits are constant drivers of their friendship, and that inclusiveness and mutual learning are key values inherent to the friendship. Xi proposed eight pragmatic cooperation initiatives in the areas of development support, food security, public health, green innovation, energy security, inter-civilizational dialogue, youth development, and security and stability to chart a path forward for building a closer China-Arab community of shared future.

The Summit issued three outcome documents: the Riyadh Declaration of the First China-Arab States Summit, the Outline of the Comprehensive Cooperation Plan Between the People's Republic of China and Arab States, and a document on Deepening the Sino-Arab Strategic Partnership for Peace and Development. They clearly stated that making an all-out effort to build a China-Arab community of shared future for the new era is the common wish and goal for China and the Arab countries alike.

China and Arab countries account for about a quarter

作为发展中国家重要成员、国际舞台上重要力量和两大文明，中阿召开首届峰会，具有超越双边和地区范畴的重大国际意义和深远历史影响，充分说明不同地区、不同文化、不同社会制度的国家完全可以相互包容借鉴、共同发展繁荣。

of the total population of the world, and they are important representatives of developing countries and important forces representing major civilizations on the international stage. The first summit between China and Arab countries exerted great international significance and far-reaching historical impact beyond the bilateral and regional scope, fully demonstrating that countries of different regions, cultures, and social systems can learn from each other and develop and prosper together.

中国—中东欧国家领导人峰会

2012年4月26日，首次中国—中东欧国家领导人会晤在波兰华沙举行，中国—中东欧国家合作正式启动。这是中国和中东欧地区国家以传统友好为底色，基于合作共赢、共谋发展的共同意愿携手打造的跨区域合作平台。中国—中东欧国家领导人峰会是这一合作机制的引领性活动。2021年2月，中国—中东欧国家领导人峰会以视频方式举行，习近平主持峰会并发表主旨讲话，精辟总结了共商共建、务实均衡、开放包容、创新进取的中国—中东欧国家合作原则。此次峰会是中国—中东欧合作机制建立以来举行的最高级别领导人会晤。

中国—中东欧国家合作参与国虽然所处地域、历史文化、发展道路和阶段不尽相同，但都能在其中各展所长，合作共赢。中国—中东欧国家合作已成为中欧关系新的增长点，也发挥着亚欧桥梁的作用。

The China-CEEC Summit

On April 26, 2012, the first China-CEEC Leaders' Meeting was held in Warsaw, Poland, marking the official launch of cooperation between China and Central and Eastern European Countries (CEEC). The summit is a cross-regional cooperation platform jointly built by China and CEEC countries based on traditional friendship and common wishes for win-win cooperation and common development. It is the pacesetting activity for the cooperation mechanism. In February 2021, the summit was held via video, with President Xi Jinping chairing the meeting and delivering a keynote speech. In the speech, he incisively summarized the principles of cooperation between China and CEEC countries such as making decisions through consultation, delivering benefits to all cooperation partners, pursuing common development through openness and inclusiveness, and achieving greater growth through innovation. This summit was the highest-level leaders' meeting since the establishment of the China-CEEC cooperation mechanism.

Although China and Central and Eastern European countries differ in terms of geography, history, culture, and development path and stage, they all have strengths to tap to achieve win-win results through cooperation. China-CEEC cooperation has become a new growth pole in China-EU relations and acts as a bridge between Asia and Europe.

中非合作论坛

在中非双方共同倡议下，中非合作论坛首届部长级会议于2000年10月在北京召开，中非合作论坛正式成立。论坛成员包括中国、53个同中国建交的非洲国家、非洲联盟委员会共55个成员。论坛迄今已举行3次峰会（2006年11月北京峰会、2015年12月约翰内斯堡峰会、2018年9月北京峰会）、7届部长级会议，制定了一系列重要的纲领性合作文件，推动实施了一系列支持非洲发展、深化中非友好互利合作的重大举措，取得丰硕成果。

习近平在2018年中非合作论坛北京峰会上全面阐述了“真、实、亲、诚”理念和正确义利观，明确了构建更加紧密的中非命运共同体的时代内涵、发展方向和前进路径，并提出了重点实施产业促进、设施联通、贸易便利、绿色发展、能力建设、健康卫生、人文交流、和平安全“八大行动”。

经过20多年的发展，论坛已成为中非开展集体对话的

Forum on China-Africa Cooperation

At the joint proposing of China and Africa, the first ministerial meeting of the Forum on China-Africa Cooperation (FOCAC) was held in Beijing in October 2000, inaugurating the forum. The forum's 55 members are China, the 53 African countries that have established diplomatic relations with China, and the African Union Commission. To date, three summits (the Beijing Summit in November 2006, the Johannesburg Summit in December 2015, and the Beijing Summit in September 2018) and seven ministerial meetings have convened. They have yielded rich results by formulating a series of important programmatic cooperation documents, promoting the implementation of a series of major measures to support Africa's development, and deepening friendly and mutually beneficial China-Africa cooperation.

At the Beijing Summit in 2018, President Xi comprehensively expounded on sincerity, real results, amity and good faith, and the principles of pursuing the greater good and shared interests. The summit clarified the heart of building a closer China-Africa community of shared future and charted a development direction and path. It also adopted eight major initiatives covering the fields of industrial promotion, infrastructure connectivity, trade facilitation, green development, capacity building, healthcare, people-to-people exchange, and peace and security.

After more than 20 years of development, the forum has become an important platform for China-Africa dialogue, an

重要平台和务实合作的有效机制，成为新时代引领国际对非合作的一面旗帜。在中非合作论坛引领下，中非高层互动日益频繁，政治互信持续深化，中非关系完成了“新型伙伴关系”“新型战略伙伴关系”“全面战略合作伙伴关系”三级跳。

effective mechanism for practical cooperation, and a bellwether for international cooperation with Africa in the new era. Largely driven by the forum, high-level interaction between China and Africa has become increasingly frequent, and political mutual trust has continued to deepen. China-Africa relations have been elevated from "a new type of partnership," to "a new type of strategic partnership" and then to "a China-Africa comprehensive strategic and cooperative partnership."

上海合作组织

上海合作组织成立于2001年6月15日，创始成员国为中国、俄罗斯、哈萨克斯坦、吉尔吉斯斯坦、塔吉克斯坦、乌兹别克斯坦。截至2023年7月，上海合作组织成员国由6个增至9个。成员国元首理事会是上海合作组织最高机构，每年举行一次例会，由轮值主席国举办，就组织内所有重大问题作出决定和指示。

上海合作组织是不同政治制度、不同文化国家和谐共处的典范。成立20多年来，上海合作组织始终遵循“互信、互利、平等、协商、尊重多样文明、谋求共同发展”的“上海精神”，致力于世界和平与发展和人类进步事业，走出了一条符合地区实际、契合各方需求的合作与发展道路，为构建新型国际关系和人类命运共同体作出重要理论和实践探索。

Shanghai Cooperation Organization

The Shanghai Cooperation Organization (SCO) was established on June 15, 2001. Its founding members were China, Russia, Kazakhstan, Kyrgyzstan, Tajikistan, and Uzbekistan. By July, 2023, the number of SCO member states has increased from 6 to 9. The Council of Heads of State is the supreme body of the SCO. It holds a regular meeting every year hosted by the rotating presidency to make decisions and instructions on major issues within the organization.

The SCO is the epitome of harmonious coexistence of countries with different political systems and cultures. Over the past 20 years since its establishment, it has always followed the "Shanghai spirit" of "mutual trust, mutual benefits, equality, consultation, respect for diverse civilizations, and pursuit of common development" and stayed committed to the cause of world peace and development and human progress. It has blazed a path of cooperation and development that conforms to regional realities and the needs of all parties and made important theoretical and practical explorations on building a new type of international relations and a global community of shared future.

金砖国家

金砖国家，因引用巴西（Brazil）、俄罗斯（Russia）、印度（India）、中国（China）、南非（South Africa）五个国家英文名称首字母组成的缩写词“BRICS”而得名。2006年，金砖国家外长举行首次会晤，开启金砖国家合作序幕。2009年，金砖国家领导人举行首次会晤，推动这一合作升级至峰会层次。2011年，南非正式加入金砖国家，金砖国家扩为五国。2023年8月，沙特、埃及、阿联酋、阿根廷、伊朗、埃塞俄比亚获邀加入金砖国家合作机制。金砖国家是全球新兴经济体的代表，在全球经济治理中捍卫广大发展中国家的利益。在金砖国家合作中，中国始终秉持开放包容、合作共赢的金砖精神，坚定不移做金砖合作的建设者和贡献者，与其他金砖国家团结协作，共同推动金砖国家高质量发展。

目前，金砖国家合作已形成以领导人会晤为引领，以安全事务高级代表会议、外长会晤等部长级会议为支撑，在经贸、财金、科技、农业、文化、教育、卫生、智库、友城等数十个领域开展务实合作的多层次架构，成为促进世界经济增长、完善全球治理、推动国际关系民主化的建设性力量。

BRICS Countries

BRICS is an acronym based on the English names of the five countries of Brazil, Russia, India, China, and South Africa. In 2006, the foreign ministers of Brazil, Russia, India, and China met for the first time, marking the beginning of BRIC cooperation. In June 2009, the BRIC leaders held their first meeting in Russia, upgrading BRIC cooperation to summit level. In 2011, South Africa officially became a member, expanding BRIC to five members and changing its name to BRICS. In August 2023, Saudi Arabia, Egypt, the United Arab Emirates (UAE), Argentina, Iran and Ethiopia were invited to join the the BRICS cooperation mechanism. BRICS countries are representatives of emerging economies, and they safeguard the interests of developing countries in global economic governance. In BRICS cooperation, China has always adhered to the BRICS spirit of openness, inclusiveness and win-win cooperation. As an unswerving builder of and contributor to BRICS cooperation, China has worked with the other BRICS countries to jointly promote the group's high-quality development.

Today, BRICS countries engage in multi-level result-oriented cooperation in dozens of fields including economics and trade, finance, science and technology, agriculture, culture, education, health, think tanks, and sister cities through a framework led by the BRICS Summit and supported by ministerial meetings such as the Meeting of BRICS High Representatives for Security Issues and the Meeting of BRICS Ministers of Foreign Affairs. The BRICS has become a major force to boost world economic growth, improve global governance, and promote democratization of international relations.

世界博览会

世界博览会，是一项由主办国政府组织或政府委托有关部门举办，有多个国家或国际组织参加，以展现人类在社会、经济、文化和科技领域取得成就的国际性大型展示会。第一届现代博览会于1851年在英国伦敦举办，集中展示世界文化与工业科技成果。2010年，上海成功举办了第41届世界博览会，这也是由中国举办的首届注册类世界博览会。上海世博会以“城市，让生活更美好”为主题，云集了246个国家和国际组织参展，接待旅客达7300多万人次，以最广泛的参与度，构成一幅多元文化和谐共融的美好画卷，有力促进了中外人文交流与民心相通。

作为最具经济与文化影响力的全球性大型盛会，世界博览会不仅汇聚了人类物质文明成果，创造了一批世界级遗产纪录，而且为人类留下了丰富的精神遗产，形成人类长久传承的共同财富。

World Expo

The World Expo is a mega international exhibition organized by a host government or relevant departments designated by the government usually attended by many countries or international organizations. The intention is to share the latest human achievements in social, economic, cultural, and scientific fields. The first World Expo was held in London in 1851 to showcase world culture and industrial, scientific and technological achievements. In 2010, Shanghai successfully hosted the 41st World Expo, the first registered World Expo held in China. Under the theme "Better City, Better Life," the Shanghai World Expo attracted 246 countries and international organizations to present exhibits and received more than 73 million visits. The heavy-participation Expo painted a beautiful picture of harmony among various cultures and effectively promoted cultural exchange between people in China and other parts of the world.

The largest global event with the most economic and cultural influence, the World Expo has not only concentrated the achievements of human material civilization with record-setting world-class heritage, but also left a rich and enduring spiritual heritage that can be passed down through generations.

世界互联网大会

世界互联网大会是由中国倡导，每年在浙江省嘉兴市桐乡乌镇举办的世界性互联网盛会，是全球互联网最新技术和前沿思想的交流平台。自2014年起，世界互联网大会乌镇峰会已连续成功举办9年，每年都有来自约80个国家和地区的千余名代表参会。2022年7月12日，世界互联网大会国际组织正式成立，旨在搭建全球互联网共商共建共享平台，推动国际社会顺应信息时代数字化、网络化、智能化趋势，共迎安全挑战，共谋发展福祉，携手构建网络空间命运共同体。

网络空间是人类共同的活动空间，网络空间前途命运应由世界各国共同掌握。世界互联网大会将“携手构建网络空间命运共同体”作为一以贯之的主题，同世界各国各地区和互联网领域各方力量一道，推动数字技术合作，完善数字环境治理，共享数字经济红利，为推动建设和平、安全、开放、合作的网络空间凝聚共识、贡献力量。

The World Internet Conference

The World Internet Conference (WIC) is an internet-themed event introduced by China and held annually in Wuzhen, Tongxiang, in Jiaxing City of Zhejiang Province. It is an exchange platform for cutting-edge internet technology and avant-garde ideas. Since 2014, the Wuzhen Summit has been held for nine consecutive years with more than 1,000 representatives from about 80 countries and regions participating every year. On July 12, 2022, the WIC international organization was officially inaugurated with an aim to build a global internet platform for joint consultation and contribution to encourage the international community to apply digital, networking, and intelligent technologies in the information era towards jointly meeting security challenges, seeking joint development, and working together to build a community with a shared future in cyberspace.

Cyberspace is a common space for human activities. The future of cyberspace should be jointly determined by all countries. The WIC will maintain its mission of "jointly building a community with a shared future in cyberspace." Alongside all countries, regions, and forces working in the internet sector, it will promote digital technology cooperation, improve governance of the digital environment, share the dividends of the digital economy, build consensus, and contribute to construction of a peaceful, safe, open, and cooperative cyberspace.

中国古代朝代对照简表

时代 / 王朝	起止时间
五帝	约前30世纪初—约前21世纪初
夏	约前2070—约前1600年
商	前1600—前1046年
周	前1046—前256年
西周	前1046—前771年
东周	前770—前256年
春秋	前770—前 476年
战国	前475—前 221年
秦	前221—前 206年
汉	前206—220年
西汉	前206—25年
东汉	25—220年
三国	220—280年
魏	220—265年
蜀	221—263年
吴	222—280年
晋	265—420年
西晋	265—317年
东晋	317—420年

CHRONOLOGY OF ANCIENT CHINESE HISTORY

PERIOD / DYNASTY	TIME SPAN
Period of the Five Legendary Rulers	c. early 30th century B.C.- c. early 21st century B.C.
Xia Dynasty	c. 2070-1600 B.C.
Shang Dynasty	1600-1046 B.C.
Zhou Dynasty	1046-256 B.C.
Western Zhou Dynasty	1046-771 B.C.
Eastern Zhou Dynasty	770-256 B.C.
Spring and Autumn Period	770-476 B.C.
Warring States Period	475-221 B.C.
Qin Dynasty	221-206 B.C.
Han Dynasty	206 B.C.-A.D. 220
Western Han Dynasty	206B.C.-A.D. 25
Eastern Han Dynasty	A.D. 25-220
Three Kingdoms	220-280
Kingdom of Wei	220-265
Kingdom of Shu	221-263
Kingdom of Wu	222-280
Jin Dynasty	265-420
Western Jin Dynasty	265-317
Eastern Jin Dynasty	317-420

时代 / 王朝	起止时间
南北朝	420—589年
南朝	420—589年
北朝	386—581年
隋	581—618年
唐	618—907年
五代十国	907—960年
宋	960—1279年
北宋	960—1127年
南宋	1127—1279年
辽	907—1125年
西夏	1038—1227年
金	1115—1234年
元	1206—1368年
明	1368—1644年
清	1616—1911年

PERIOD / DYNASTY	TIME SPAN
Northern and Southern Dynasties	420-589
Southern Dynasties	420-589
Northern Dynasties	386-581
Sui Dynasty	581-618
Tang Dynasty	618-907
Five Dynasties and Ten Kingdoms	907-960
Song Dynasty	960-1279
Northern Song Dynasty	960-1127
Southern Song Dynasty	1127-1279
Liao Dynasty	907-1125
Xixia Dynasty	1038-1227
Jin Dynasty	1115-1234
Yuan Dynasty	1206-1368
Ming Dynasty	1368-1644
Qing Dynasty	1616-1911

词条音序排列表

ENTRIES IN ALPHABETICAL ORDER

图书在版编目（CIP）数据

中国关键词. 文明互鉴篇 : 汉英对照 / 中国外文出
版发行事业局, 当代中国与世界研究院, 中国翻译研究院
著 ; 王海荣, 杜楠, 宋晗阳译. -- 北京 : 朝华出版社
2023.8
ISBN 978-7-5054-5237-4
Ⅰ. ①中… Ⅱ. ①中… ②当… ③中… ④王… ⑤杜
… ⑥宋… Ⅲ. ①中国特色社会主义—社会主义建设模式
—研究—汉、英②中外关系—文化交流—研究—汉、英
Ⅳ. ①D616②G125
中国国家版本馆CIP数据核字(2023)第063273号

中国关键词：文明互鉴篇（汉英对照）

作　　者	中国外文出版发行事业局　当代中国与世界研究院 中国翻译研究院
英文翻译	王海荣　杜　楠　宋晗阳
英文改稿	Scott Huntsman [美]
英文审定	贺　军
特约编辑/项目统筹	申　阳
项目执行	华光灿
翻译统筹	赵维真　王蕴航
责任编辑	赵　倩　张北鱼
责任印制	陆竞赢　崔　航
装帧设计	杜　帅
出版发行	朝华出版社
社　　址	北京西城区百万庄大街24号　**邮政编码**　100037
出版合作	（010）68995532
订购电话	（010）68996522
传　　真	（010）88415258（发行部）
联系版权	zhbq@cicg.org.cn
网　　址	http: //zhcb.cicg.org.cn
印　　刷	天津中印联印务有限公司
经　　销	全国新华书店
开　　本	880mm×1230mm　1 / 32　　**字　　数**　60千字
印　　张	6.75
版　　次	2023年8月第1版　2023年8月第1次印刷
装　　别	平
书　　号	ISBN 978-7-5054-5237-4
定　　价	68.00元